# THE VIKINGS & THE CELTS
## ANCIENT WARRIORS AND FIERCE RAIDERS

Discover the dramatic world of the Celts and Vikings
with how-to projects and 700 pictures

**FIONA MACDONALD AND PHILIP STEELE**
**Consultants: Lloyd Laing, Nottingham University
and Leslie Webster, British Museum**

southwater

This edition is published by Southwater, an imprint of Anness Publishing Ltd, Hermes House,
88–89 Blackfriars Road, London SE1 8HA; tel. 020 7401 2077; fax 020 7633 9499

www.southwaterbooks.com; www.annesspublishing.com

Anness Publishing has a new picture agency outlet for images for publishing, promotions or advertising.
Please visit our website www.practicalpictures.com for more information.

UK agent: The Manning Partnership Ltd; tel. 01225 478444; fax 01225 478440; sales@manning-partnership.co.uk
UK distributor: Book Trade Services; tel. 0116 2759086; fax 0116 2759090; uksales@booktradeservices.com;
exportsales@booktradeservices.com
North American agent/distributor: National Book Network; tel. 301 459 3366; fax 301 429 5746; www.nbnbooks.com
Australian agent/distributor: Pan Macmillan Australia; tel. 1300 135 113; fax 1300 135 103;
customer.service@macmillan.com.au
New Zealand agent/distributor: David Bateman Ltd; tel. (09) 415 7664; fax (09) 415 8892

Publisher: Joanna Lorenz
Managing Editor, Children's Books: Gilly Cameron Cooper
Senior Editor: Nicole Pearson
Copy Editors: Nicola Barber, Louisa Somerville
Designers: Simon Borrough, Caroline Reeves
Illustration: Rob Ashby, Julian Baker, Vanessa Card, Stuart Carter, Shane Marsh
Special Photography: John Freeman
Stylist: Thomasina Smith

ETHICAL TRADING POLICY

Because of our ongoing ecological investment programme, you, as our customer, can have the pleasure and reassurance
of knowing that a tree is being cultivated on your behalf to naturally replace the materials used to make the book
you are holding. For further information about this scheme, go to www.annesspublishing.com/trees

Previously published as *Raiders of the North*

PUBLISHER'S NOTE

Although the advice and information in this book are believed to be accurate and true at the time of going to press, neither the
authors nor the publisher can accept any legal responsibility or liability for any errors or omissions that may be made nor for
any inaccuracies nor for any harm or injury that comes about from following instructions or advice in this book.

Anness Publishing would like to thank the following children for modelling for this book: Hazel Askew, Christopher
Aurokium, Anthony Bainbridge, Sarah Bone, Christopher Brown, Jessica Castenada, Liliana Conceicao de Jesus, Louise
Gannon, Bobbi Graham, Karrine Gray, Eleanor Grimshaw, Daniel Haston, Isha Janneh, Eka Karumidze, Mohsin Laher,
Muhammed Laher, Victoria Lebedeva, Artem Lissovets, Bianca S. Loucaides, Rebecca Miah, Gabriel Nipah,
Daniel A. Otalvora, Sarah Phillips, Charlie Emilin Ray, Tom Swaine-Jameson, Arkam Udoh.

# CONTENTS

# WARRIOR PEOPLES

THE CELTS AND VIKINGS are often thought of as warrior peoples. They certainly liked to tell stories about their battles, raids and daring deeds, and many of them were brave warriors. However, no people can live just by fighting. The Celts and the Vikings made ploughs as well as swords. They farmed and fished. They were weavers of fine cloth and makers of beautiful jewellery of gold and silver. Both peoples were also expert at working with iron.

The Celts first made their mark on the European way of life about 2,750 years ago, while the Vikings stormed their way into history some 1,500 years later. Through trade, migration and exploration, both peoples spread far and wide. Their descendants still live in north-western Europe, Scandinavia and many other parts of the world today.

### A Superstitious People

Epona was a war goddess worshipped by Celts in France and later in Britain. The ancient Celts and the Vikings worshipped many gods. Religion was particularly important in the lives of the Celts. A large number of statues of their gods and goddesses have survived until today.

### The Celtic Homelands

Originally, the Celtic people came from Central Europe (the areas shown in orange and yellow on the map) but their way of life was adopted by other peoples. They also raided and settled many new lands. At its greatest extent, the Celtic world stretched from Spain to Turkey, and from northern Italy to Scotland.

### A Celtic Roundhouse

The western Celts built roundhouses. These were thatched and built of local materials, such as wood, or sometimes stone. Around the inside of the house were compartments made of wickerwork, with a large space for cooking and eating in the upper storey. Dwellings were often shared with the farm animals, particularly during the cold winter months.

## A VIKING FORT

The Danish Vikings built fortifications like this on the islands of Fyn and Sjaelland and also in Jutland. These forts were probably raised in the late AD900s. At this time, bands of unruly Vikings led by local chiefs were beginning to come under the rule of powerful Scandinavian kings. Originally, the Vikings had organized themselves in local groups, loyal to a chief. However, over time, countries were united and ruled by a single king.

## THE VIKING HOMELANDS

The Vikings were Germanic peoples who lived in Scandinavia. They raided and settled large areas of Europe, and reached Russia, Arabia and North America.

## LONGSHIP ON THE HORIZON

With its dragon-headed prow dipping through the waves, a Viking warship cuts through the sea. People all over Europe dreaded hearing the words 'the Vikings are coming'. During the AD800s, the Vikings terrorized coastal settlements around the North Sea, the Irish Sea and the English Channel.

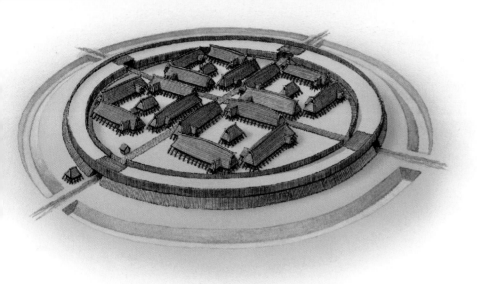

## HORSEBACK HERO

A Celtic warrior rides into battle. Acts of individual heroism were much admired by both the Celts and the Vikings. However, the Celts were no match for the ruthless and disciplined invading armies of the Roman Empire.

# THE
# CELTS

The ancient Greeks gave the name Celts to the northern tribes who raided their lands. Although the Celts were warriors, they were also hardworking farmers and remarkable craftsmen.

by
FIONA MACDONALD
Consultant: Lloyd Laing,
Nottingham University

# The Ancient Celts

FROM AROUND 750BC TO 12BC, the Celts were the most powerful people in central and northern Europe. There were many groups (sometimes called tribes) of Celts. They spoke related languages, shared similar, but not identical, technologies, customs and beliefs, and created works of art in closely connected styles. Their civilization flourished across a vast area, from the British Isles to the borders of Ukraine. However, there was never one single Celtic nation, language or lifestyle. Celtic traditions developed at different times and in different places. The Celts also borrowed many ideas and designs from other European peoples, including the Greeks, the Etruscans and Romans (from Italy), and the Scythians (from the Black Sea area).

### WAR-MAD?
This bronze statue of a Celtic warrior god has fierce, staring eyes of shiny glass paste. It was made in France during the 1st century BC. Around the time the statue was created, the Greek geographer Strabo described the Celts as 'war-mad ... high-spirited and quick for battle'.

### MYSTERIOUS GOD
An unknown Celtic god is portrayed in this stone statue from France. Similar statues made from stone or wood stood in the Celts' most holy shrines. The god has a wild boar on his chest, and round his neck he wears a torc (heavy necklace). The Celts believed that torcs had magic power.

## TIMELINE c.800–400BC

*Celtic civilization flourished from about 750BC to 12BC, but some Celtic ideas, beliefs and traditions continued in north-west Europe for another 700 years.*

c.800–600BC Groups of horsemen with long iron swords and wheeled chariots become powerful in central Europe.

c.800–600BC New defences are built

*example of early Celtic metalwork*

around many European villages, probably to defend them from Celtic attack. At the same time, long-distance trade is disrupted, and production of fine craftwork slows down.

c.750–500BC The new technology of ironworking becomes popular in central Europe.

*rucksack from the salt mines in Hallstatt*

c.700–450BC The miners, merchants, craftworkers and soldiers living in and around the salt mines at Hallstatt, Austria, become rich and powerful. Their salt is traded throughout central Europe. It is highly prized for preserving food and as medicine for cattle.

c.700–450BC The Hallstatt people are ruled by Celtic warrior families; they can afford new iron weapons, as well as fine bronze vessels and gold jewellery.

*Celtic farmers*

c.800BC          750BC          700BC          650BC          600BC

## SIMPLE SCRIPT

The Celts had no written script of their own. For important monuments, such as this standing stone from Ireland, they borrowed scripts used by neighbouring peoples. This inscription is carved in Ogham – a script based on the Roman alphabet, but using lines instead of letters. It is difficult to discover everything we would like to know about the Celts because they did not keep detailed written records.

## METALWORK

The Celts were famous throughout Europe for their skill as metalworkers. This bronze disc was made to decorate a horse harness in about 450BC. It was found by archaeologists in a Celtic burial site in France. Archaeologists have been investigating the remains of Celtic civilization, such as burial sites, for over 200 years. During that time, they have made many remarkable discoveries, including rich tombs and beautiful jewellery.

## KEY

◆ Hallstatt culture (750–450BC)

◆ La Tène culture (450–50BC)

## THE CELTIC HEARTLANDS

This map shows the parts of Europe where archaeologists have found some of the best-preserved evidence for Celtic culture. The Hallstatt region of Austria was the richest, most powerful part of the Celtic lands from around 750 to 450BC. Later, from around 450 to 50BC, the La Tène region of Switzerland became one of the leading centres of the Celtic civilization.

---

c.600–500BC Celtic warrior-princes rule in Europe, from central France to the borders of present-day Hungary. They build citadels (fortified towns) on high land overlooking the countryside and establish trade routes under their control.

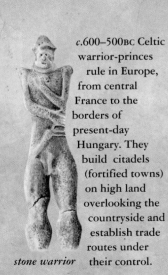

*stone warrior*

c.520BC A 35-year-old woman is buried in a wood-lined chamber at Vix in eastern France. Alongside her are personal ornaments, a dismantled burial wagon and imported drinking vessels. The woman wears a massive torc around her neck containing almost half a kilo of pure gold.

*Vix krater
(wine serving bowl)*

c.500BC Celtic society becomes more equal. Warrior princes abandon their citadels and live closer to farmers, traders and craftworkers. Celtic culture reaches Brittany and possibly as far as parts of northern Spain.

c.450BC La Tène style of art develops in central Europe producing some of the finest Celtic art objects.

*La Tène statue*

550BC          500BC          450BC          400BC

# The Celtic World

The story of the Celts begins between 750BC and 600BC. At this time, Celtic warrior chieftains began to ride on horseback and to arm themselves with long swords. When they died, they were buried in magnificent tombs containing wagons with iron-rimmed wheels and sumptuous gold jewellery. These extravagant burials tell us that the Celtic peoples were both powerful and wealthy. The Celts' power came from their strength as horse-riding warriors. They became wealthy from the profitable salt and copper mines around Hallstatt in Austria, and from the trade in valuable goods and raw materials (such as iron ore) with peoples who lived further south. By around 550BC, the Celts were building citadels (fortified towns) to dominate the surrounding land.

The years from 400BC to 200BC were a time of migrations. Celts moved northwards to Germany and southwards to Italy. In 350BC, they invaded western Hungary, then headed south into Greece. In 279BC they attacked the Greeks' holiest shrine, the temple of Apollo at Delphi, but were driven away. Another group of Celts settled in Turkey around 240BC. At the same time, Celtic peoples moved into south-western France, Spain and Portugal. This brought them face to face with the Roman army – the strongest fighting force in Europe. For the next 200 years, Romans and Celts were at war. By around AD60, Celtic power was almost completely destroyed. Only in remote areas such as Brittany, Scotland, Ireland and Wales did Celtic traditions survive.

ATLANTIC OCEAN

*Oppidum (fortif town) of Citania de Sanfins*

*Iberian fortified settle*

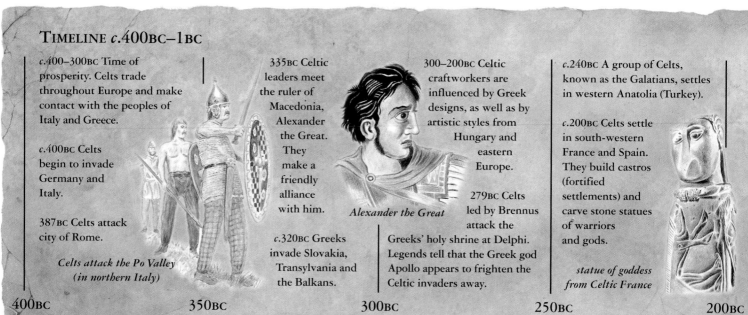

## TIMELINE *c.*400BC–1BC

*c.*400–300BC Time of prosperity. Celts trade throughout Europe and make contact with the peoples of Italy and Greece.

*c.*400BC Celts begin to invade Germany and Italy.

387BC Celts attack city of Rome.

*Celts attack the Po Valley (in northern Italy)*

335BC Celtic leaders meet the ruler of Macedonia, Alexander the Great. They make a friendly alliance with him.

*c.*320BC Greeks invade Slovakia, Transylvania and the Balkans.

*Alexander the Great*

300–200BC Celtic craftworkers are influenced by Greek designs, as well as by artistic styles from Hungary and eastern Europe.

279BC Celts led by Brennus attack the Greeks' holy shrine at Delphi. Legends tell that the Greek god Apollo appears to frighten the Celtic invaders away.

*c.*240BC A group of Celts, known as the Galatians, settles in western Anatolia (Turkey).

*c.*200BC Celts settle in south-western France and Spain. They build castros (fortified settlements) and carve stone statues of warriors and gods.

*statue of goddess from Celtic France*

400BC      350BC      300BC      250BC      200BC

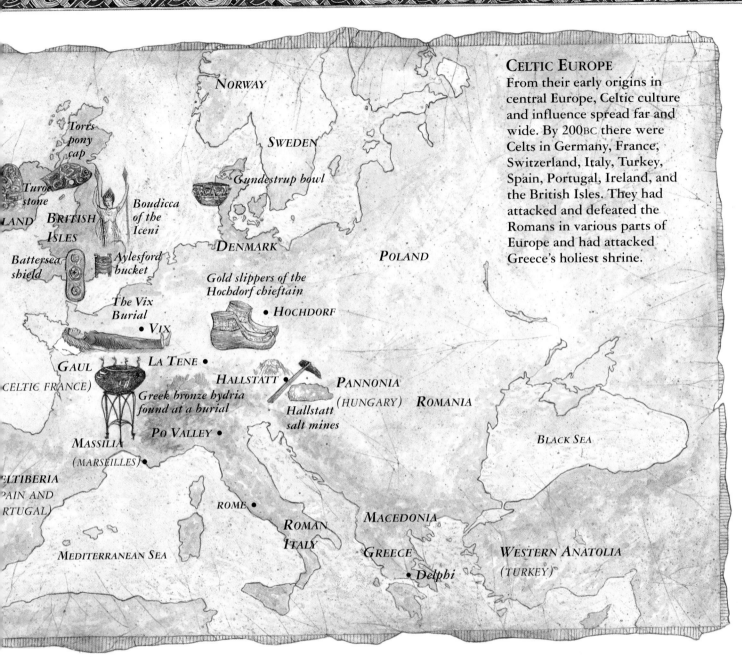

**CELTIC EUROPE**
From their early origins in central Europe, Celtic culture and influence spread far and wide. By 200BC there were Celts in Germany, France, Switzerland, Italy, Turkey, Spain, Portugal, Ireland, and the British Isles. They had attacked and defeated the Romans in various parts of Europe and had attacked Greece's holiest shrine.

Map labels:
- NORWAY
- SWEDEN
- DENMARK
- POLAND
- Torrs pony cap
- Turoe stone
- BRITISH ISLES
- Boudicca of the Iceni
- Battersea shield
- Aylesford bucket
- Gundestrup bowl
- Gold slippers of the Hochdorf chieftain
- HOCHDORF
- The Vix Burial
- VIX
- GAUL (CELTIC FRANCE)
- LA TENE
- Greek bronze hydria found at a burial
- HALLSTATT
- Hallstatt salt mines
- PANNONIA (HUNGARY)
- ROMANIA
- BLACK SEA
- PO VALLEY
- MASSILIA (MARSEILLES)
- CELTIBERIA (SPAIN AND PORTUGAL)
- ROME
- ROMAN ITALY
- MACEDONIA
- GREECE
- Delphi
- WESTERN ANATOLIA (TURKEY)
- MEDITERRANEAN SEA

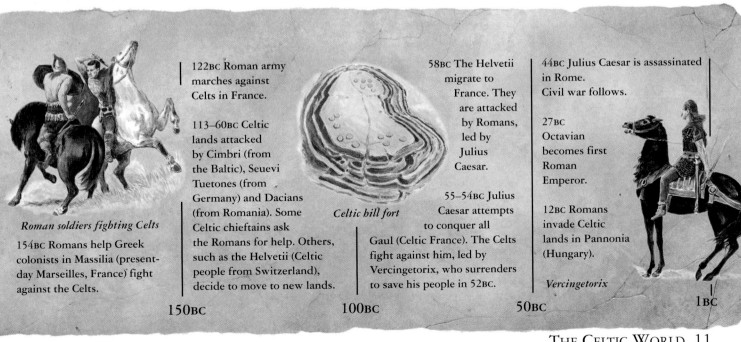

*Roman soldiers fighting Celts*

154BC Romans help Greek colonists in Massilia (present-day Marseilles, France) fight against the Celts.

122BC Roman army marches against Celts in France.

113–60BC Celtic lands attacked by Cimbri (from the Baltic), Seuevi Tuetones (from Germany) and Dacians (from Romania). Some Celtic chieftains ask the Romans for help. Others, such as the Helvetii (Celtic people from Switzerland), decide to move to new lands.

*Celtic hill fort*

58BC The Helvetii migrate to France. They are attacked by Romans, led by Julius Caesar.

55–54BC Julius Caesar attempts to conquer all Gaul (Celtic France). The Celts fight against him, led by Vercingetorix, who surrenders to save his people in 52BC.

44BC Julius Caesar is assassinated in Rome. Civil war follows.

27BC Octavian becomes first Roman Emperor.

12BC Romans invade Celtic lands in Pannonia (Hungary).

*Vercingetorix*

150BC        100BC        50BC        1BC

# Famous Celts

EVEN THOUGH THE CELTS did not keep written records, we know the names of some people who lived in Celtic times. This is because people who could read and write, such as Greek geographers and Roman army commanders, described some of the Celtic leaders they came across. To the Celts themselves, being respected was more important than life itself. The legendary Irish hero, Cuchulainn, was reported to have said: 'So long as I am famous, I do not care if I live for just one day in this world.' The qualities that the Celts most admired were bravery, wealth and generosity. Rulers who owned rich treasures and wore magnificent jewels were admired for bringing honour to their tribe by their glittering display of wealth. Fierce war-leaders such as Boudicca, Cunobelinus and Vercingetorix were praised for their courage and bravery when faced with death. Even after Celtic power faded away, adventurous missionaries such as St Columba worked to win fame for the Christian faith.

**BURIED TREASURE**
This Celtic princess was buried at Vix, in eastern France, around 520BC. Her tomb is one of the most splendid ever discovered in Europe, and contained rich treasures from as far away as Greece. The princess was wearing a torc made of almost half a kilogram of pure gold.

**HERO OF FRANCE**
Vercingetorix led the Gauls (the Celtic people of France) in their last fight against the Romans in 52BC. He bravely surrendered in order to allow his followers to escape death.

## TIMELINE AD1–1066

AD1 End of Celtic power in mainland Europe. Celtic traditions continue in isolated regions, such as Brittany.

AD43 Romans conquer southern Britain.

*Boudicca*

AD60 Queen Boudicca of the Celtic Iceni tribe (from eastern England) leads a rebellion against the Romans.

AD61 Boudicca is defeated. End of Celtic power in England.

AD122 Roman emperor, Hadrian, builds a wall across northern England to defend Roman lands from Celts to the north. Celtic culture mingles with, and is largely absorbed by, Roman

*Hadrian's Wall*

culture in southern Britain. Celtic influence continues, in part, in Scotland, Wales and Ireland. Descendants of Celtic chiefs continue to rule in these three areas.

AD410 Romans withdraw from Britain.

AD432 Christian missionary, St Patrick, brings the Christian faith to Ireland. From now on, Irish monks copy Celtic traditions, especially in art. They also help to preserve ancient Celtic stories and beliefs by writing them down in manuscripts.

*a Christian saint*

AD1                                                 AD250                                                 AD500

## BRITISH KING

This beautiful gold coin was made for Cunobelinus, one of the last Celtic chieftains. He ruled lands in south-east England from around AD10 to AD40. His sons led the Celtic fight against the Roman conquerors of Britain.

## CELTIC SAINT

St Columba was born into a Celtic family in Ireland in AD521. He became a Christian monk and spent many years preaching in Ireland. In AD563 he went to Scotland where he founded a monastery on the island of Iona. From there, he and his monks took news of the Christian faith to the peoples of Scotland.

## WARRIOR QUEEN

Boudicca was wife of the ruler of the Iceni, a Celtic people who lived in eastern England. After her husband's death, the Romans claimed the Iceni lands. When Boudicca protested she was beaten and her daughters raped. In revenge, Boudicca led an army to attack London in AD60–1. Boudicca's army caused vast amounts of damage before being defeated.

AD500 onwards Britain is invaded by Angles and Saxons. They introduce a new Germanic language and culture.

c.AD560 Irish monks re-introduce Celtic artistic traditions to England, along with their Christian religious teachings. They decorate Christian texts and monuments with swirling Celtic designs.

AD563–597 The Christian missionary, St Columba, sets up a monastery on the island of Iona, off the west coast of Scotland. It becomes a centre of Christian, Celtic art and learning.

*the Book of Durrow*

AD675 *Book of Durrow* is written in the monastery at Durrow reputedly by St Columba himself.

c.AD790 First Viking raid on Britain. The Vikings introduce their own language and culture.

c.AD800 *Book of Kells* is produced in Ireland. It is one of the last masterpieces of late Celtic art. It contains the Christian Gospels as well as Irish texts.

*a Celtic cross*

1066 Normans (Vikings who had settled in France) invade Britain. Last traces of Celtic culture disappear in British Isles. But a few traces remain in folk songs, myths and legends, and in the Gaelic, Welsh, Cornish and Manx languages.

AD750

AD1000

# Origins and Migration

Historians used to think that the Celts were a single ethnic group who originated in one place, north of the Black Sea, then spread across Europe. However, this view has since been challenged. Most experts now believe that the Celts were descended from earlier inhabitants of northern Europe. They also think that the Celts were not one ethnic group, but many different peoples who shared a similar way of life that changed and developed over the centuries between around 800BC and AD100.

There were some major movements (migrations) of Celtic tribes, mostly from Celtic lands to non-Celtic countries in Europe. In about 400BC, it seems that some parts of France became overcrowded. Celtic warriors, farmers and their families set out towards Germany and Italy. One group settled south of the Alps, on fertile land in northern Italy. In 350BC, more Celtic migrants moved into western Hungary, Slovakia and Transylvania. Soon afterwards, they headed southwards into Greece and Bulgaria. There is not much evidence to suggest that there were large-scale migrations from mainland Europe into the British Isles. It seems that local Celtic civilization developed independently in Britain. There were also many links between British, Irish and European Celtic peoples through long-distance trade.

**TYPICAL LA TÈNE**
Historians divide the Celtic age into two main sections, the Hallstatt era (from about 750BC to 450BC) and the La Tène era (from about 450BC to 50BC). Both eras are named after types of Celtic art. Fine metalwork and rich burials are typical of the Hallstatt era. Elaborate, swirling designs, such as the ones on this carved stone pillar, are typical of the art of the La Tène era.

**RICHES FROM SALT**
This drawing of a Hallstatt burial was made in about 1860. Over 2,000 burials have been discovered at the Austrian town of Hallstatt, most dating from 800–600BC. Around 800BC, the Celts living near Hallstatt began to grow rich and powerful because they controlled the salt trade. They buried their dead with precious goods such as jewellery and daggers.

## ART FROM THE EAST

This bronze harness mount was made in Ukraine in about AD100. It shows that Celtic designs were popular on the eastern frontiers of Europe, and that Celtic metalworking skills were also known there. Like many pieces of Celtic art, it is decorated with patterns based on spiral shapes.

## IRON AND SALT

The Celts discovered how to mine and process the iron ore and salt in their lands. They exchanged iron objects and salt for goods with merchants from all over Europe. Iron ore (left) and rock salt (right) were very valuable commodities. Iron was used to make sharp, long-lasting weapons and tools, and it also had prestige value. Salt was used in medicines and to preserve food.

*iron ore*        *rock salt*

## MOUNTED HUNTER

At the beginning of the Hallstatt era (750–450BC), big, strong horses were introduced into western Europe from the lands east of the Black Sea. These mounts gave Celtic hunters and warriors a great advantage. This bronze statue shows a Celtic hunter on horseback, mounted on a burial wagon.

## A SHARED STYLE

Wherever they lived in Europe, Celtic craftworkers decorated the objects they made using similar styles and techniques. This pottery vessel was made in about 350BC. It is decorated with lines scratched into the clay. The pattern featured on the vessel is also found on metalwork created during the period.

## A LASTING TRADITION

Celtic art styles remained popular for centuries after Celtic power faded away, especially in the British Isles. This bronze attachment from a silver reliquary (container for holy objects) was made in Ireland in about AD700.

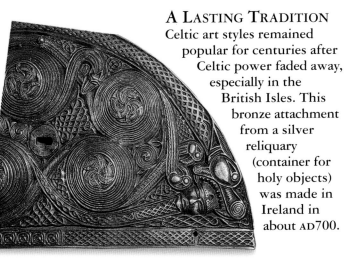

# The Decline of the Celts

CELTIC POWER in Europe lasted for around 800 years. As it declined, Celtic lands were divided among many other peoples who had grown strong enough to make their own claims for power. The first people to fight against the Celts were also the most formidable – the well-trained, well-equipped soldiers of the Roman empire. The Romans managed to drive the Celtic settlers out of northern Italy in 191BC. They took control of Spain in 133BC and, after long campaigns led by the brilliant general, Julius Caesar, finally conquered France in 51BC. Roman armies invaded southern Britain in AD43. At first there was resistance, such as the revolt led by the Celtic queen, Boudicca. Nevertheless, by AD61 the Romans controlled southern Britain, and they ruled there until AD410. However, the Romans never managed to conquer all the British Isles. Parts of Scotland and Ireland continued under Celtic rule until about AD1100. As Roman power weakened, new groups of migrants arrived, mostly from the north, to settle in the former Celtic lands. These invaders included many peoples with strong armies and vibrant cultures of their own, such as the Visigoths, the Angles and Saxons, the Franks, and the Vikings.

## GREAT CONQUEROR
Julius Caesar (c.100–44BC) led the Roman armies that conquered the Celts in France. He fought and won a series of battles, known as the Gallic Wars, between 58BC and 51BC. He also hoped to conquer Britain and Germany, but a political crisis in Italy forced him to return to Rome.

## ROMAN STYLE
After the Romans conquered Britain in AD43, a new, mixed civilization grew up which combined both Roman and Celtic traditions. Although some Celtic chieftains rebelled against Roman rule, others decided to co-operate with the Romans, and served as local governors. They built splendid country houses, known as villas, which were decorated in the Roman style with beautiful mosaic floors such as this one.

## THE VISIGOTHS

This jewelled, golden crown was made for the Visigothic kings of Spain to give as a religious offering. The Visigoths were a people from northern Europe. Celtic lands in Spain were conquered by the Romans in 133BC, and then by the Visigoths in about AD400. Even so, many Celtic skills, such as the art of fine metalworking, survived and were passed down by successive generations of settlers.

## KING OF THE FRANKS

The Romans ruled France until about AD400. Northern France was then taken over by the Franks, a people from southern Germany. The Frankish kings built up a powerful empire in former Celtic France. Their most successful and powerful ruler was King Charlemagne (left), who reigned from AD771 to 814.

## VIKING WARRIORS

The Vikings were sailors, raiders and traders who came from Scandinavia. They first attacked Britain around AD790. Soon afterwards, Viking settlers came to live in many parts of the British Isles and northern France. This tombstone shows two Viking warriors with round shields.

## SAXON KING

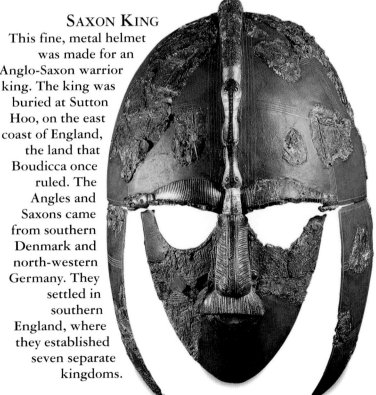

This fine, metal helmet was made for an Anglo-Saxon warrior king. The king was buried at Sutton Hoo, on the east coast of England, the land that Boudicca once ruled. The Angles and Saxons came from southern Denmark and north-western Germany. They settled in southern England, where they established seven separate kingdoms.

# Tribes and Clans

THE CELTS WERE NEVER a single, unified nation. Instead there were many separate Celtic tribes throughout Europe. Greek and Roman writers recorded many Celtic tribal names, for example, the Helvetii (who lived in Switzerland) and the Caledones (who lived in Scotland). Tribes sometimes made friendly alliances with one another, or with a stronger power such as Rome. This usually happened when a tribe was threatened by invaders or at war. Within each tribe, there were many clans. These were families who traced their descent from a single ancestor, and who shared ties of loyalty and a family name.

Each tribe was headed by a king (or chieftain). His task was to lead men in battle and on raids, and to maintain peace and prosperity. Kings were chosen from rich noble families. Senior noblemen were expected to support the king and to lead their own bands of warriors. Druids (Celtic priests) and bards (well-educated poets) also came from noble families. Farmers and craftworkers ranked lower, but they were highly valued for their important skills. There were also servants and slaves.

## GUARDIAN GODDESS
Many Celtic tribes had their own special god or goddess, to protect them and to bring fertility to their farm animals and crops. This mother goddess was the special guardian of a Celtic tribe who lived in Austria. She is shown gently cradling twin babies on her lap – a vivid reminder of her magical protective powers. After a battle, the Celts sacrificed a share of all they had captured to their favourite gods and goddesses.

## PROUD LEADER
This stone statue portrays a Celtic king or chieftain from Gaul (present-day France). It was made around 50BC. He is dressed ready to lead his tribe into war, in a chain mail tunic and a magic torc. His torc is an indication of high rank, but we have no idea who he actually was.

## THE STRUCTURE OF SOCIETY

All the different groups within Celtic society had an important part to play, and they all relied on one another to survive. This diagram shows what each different group gave to society, and what it received in return. Chieftains offered leadership and inspired loyalty, while nobles and warriors protected the tribe from attack. Druids and bards provided religious support and celebrated tribal pride. Farmers and craftworkers produced food and goods. The lowest social rank was held by labourers and slaves. They did jobs that were often hard and dirty.

*Religious support knowledge, rituals*

*Protection and offerings*

*Gifts and prestige*

*Loyalty and help in battle*

*Chieftains*

Protection and offerings

Religious support

*Farmers and craftworkers*

*Druids and bards*

*Nobles and warriors*

*Religious support*

*Respect and offerings*

*Respect and manpower*

*Protection and access to land*

## TRIBAL COIN

Many Celtic tribes issued coins, marked with their own special design. This coin was made for the Catuvellauni tribe who lived in southern England. It shows a warrior on horseback riding into battle brandishing a carnyx (war-trumpet). It was designed to tell everyone what a brave and warlike people the Catuvellauni were.

## SLAVE CHAIN

Chains like these were used to stop slaves running away. The round iron bracelets, joined by links of heavy metal, were fastened round a slave's wrists or ankles and locked shut. Slavery was never very important in Celtic society. There were many more free people than slaves. However, slaves were used for dirty, difficult, dangerous work (for example, in the salt mines at Hallstatt).

# Hero Chieftains

STRENGTH, BOLDNESS, boastfulness, courage – these were the qualities that made a Celtic hero. Brave Celtic warriors often fought as individual champions, parading in front of the enemy before a battle, boasting of their brave deeds and those of their ancestors, and daring anyone to fight against them. Chieftains might also be accompanied to the battlefield by a parasite, the name for a low-ranking follower who had the task of praising the chieftain and his exploits in war. Sometimes, a war was settled by two hero chieftains fighting one another.

All Celtic warriors knew that a battle might well lead to death, but they did not show fear. This was partly because bands of warriors worked themselves up into a state of fury as they prepared for a fight, to give each other courage. They also drank large amounts of strong ale or wine. The din of drums and war-trumpets may have helped to induce a trance-like state. The Celts' beliefs helped them face death and danger, too. Celtic people thought that their spirits would not die, even though their bodies were killed. They believed that it was better to die in battle than to survive and face defeat. Defeat led to deep disgrace, and often suicide.

### ELITE WARRIOR
A Celtic warrior hero from Germany is portrayed in this sandstone statue from around 550BC. The warrior wears a torc and a sword-belt. His conical helmet would have been made of metal. Similar helmets have been found in the graves of many Celtic warriors.

### A NOBLE DEATH
This famous statue, known as the *Dying Gaul*, presents a noble portrait of an injured Celtic chief as he endures suffering and awaits death. Battle wounds were a source of pride. A warrior who survived a fight might make his own injuries worse if they did not look very impressive.

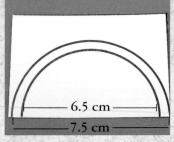

### MAKE A HELMET
*You will need: bowl, PVA glue, water, newspaper, balloon, petroleum jelly, pair of compasses, felt-tip pen, card 17cm x 8cm, ruler, scissors, gold and bronze paint, paintbrushes, dowelling.*

**1** To make papier-mâché, fill the bowl with 1 part PVA glue to 3 parts water. Tear up the newspaper and soak the pieces in the glue and water mixture.

**2** Blow up the balloon to the size of your head and cover with petroleum jelly. Build up papier-mâché layers on the top and sides of the balloon.

6.5 cm
7.5 cm

**3** Use compasses to draw a semicircle on the card 7.5cm in diameter. In the same way, draw another semicircle 6.5cm in diameter inside the first.

## WARRIOR ON WHEELS

After around 450BC, Celtic warriors were buried in lightweight, two-wheeled chariots, just like the chariots they drove into battle. Their weapons and drinking bowls were arranged beside them as well. This warrior's grave was discovered in northern France.

## BRAVE SACRIFICE

A Celtic warrior commits suicide after killing his wife. This marble statue was created after the Gauls (migrating Celts from France) had been defeated by King Attalus I of Pergamon, Asia Minor, in 230BC. Roman writers reported that the Celts would choose death rather than spend the rest of their lives in captivity, or suffering from the dishonour of defeat.

## HALLSTATT HELMET

This pointed metal helmet was found near Salzburg, in Austria, not far from the Hallstatt salt mines. It was buried in a warrior's grave during the La Tène era (450–50BC). Compare it with the helmet worn by the stone warrior in the statue on the opposite page.

*The original helmet that inspired the design for your model was found in northern France. It was decorated with gold, which sparkled in the sun.*

**4** Draw lines at intervals in-between the two semicircles. Cut around the inner semicircle. Cut rounded corners off the top of the card, as shown.

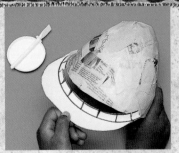

**5** When the papier-mâché helmet is dry, pop the balloon. Trim the helmet. Next, cut into the tabs on the peak. Glue the peak in position, as shown.

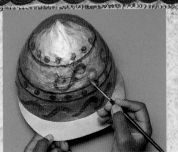

**6** Paint all of the peak and helmet with gold paint and allow to dry. Then decorate with the bronze paint, using Celtic designs, as shown.

**7** Finally, use the small piece of dowelling to add the finishing touches to your helmet. Place in a warm place until it is completely dry.

# Head-hunting Raiders

**R**AIDING WAS AN ESSENTIAL PART of Celtic life. Bands of young, male warriors regularly rode off to attack and plunder neighbouring Celts or more distant foreign peoples. Raiding was the way for a man to win praise and to demonstrate his skill and bravery. It also increased his status within the community by attracting groups of loyal followers. These followers helped, supported and obeyed him in return for gifts and protection from attack.

Raids might last for a few hours or a few months, but their purpose was always the same. The aim was to win rich prizes such as captives, precious goods, animals or food. These were shared out by the raider among his followers, friends and relatives at a great feast. The more gifts the raider gave, the higher his prestige, and the more followers he could attract. The Celts also saw raiding as an enjoyable sport and as good training for war. On raids, Celtic warriors practised skills that would be useful on a battlefield, such as fighting with swords and spears, and horse riding.

Some historians think that the habit of making long-distance raids encouraged the Celts to start spreading across Europe. The Celtic migrations began in about 400BC, possibly because the Celts had run out of people to attack and lands to conquer nearer home.

### SEVERED HEAD
After raids and battles, Celtic warriors might return home carrying the heads of enemies they had killed. They would nail these heads to the doors of their houses as trophies. It seems clear that heads had a special, religious or magic meaning for the Celts, but historians are not exactly sure what this was. Most think that, for the Celts, the head was the site of a person's spirit and power.

### ON THE RUN
Made around 175BC, this Roman stone carving shows two Celtic warriors dropping the plunder they have seized on a raid. They are in a hurry to escape because they are being chased by angry enemies. The carving is part of a Roman monument celebrating the defeat of the Celts in northern Italy by Roman troops. The Roman stone-carver has shown the Celts as naked 'barbarians'. However, it is almost certain that the Celts went raiding with their clothes on.

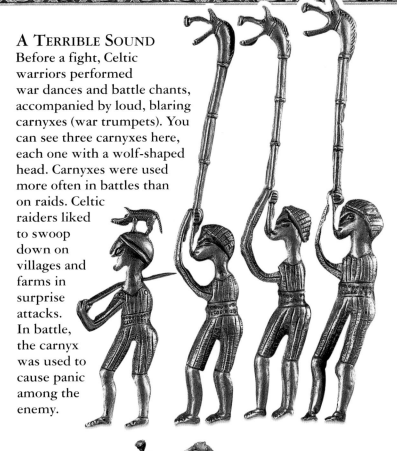

## A TERRIBLE SOUND

Before a fight, Celtic warriors performed war dances and battle chants, accompanied by loud, blaring carnyxes (war trumpets). You can see three carnyxes here, each one with a wolf-shaped head. Carnyxes were used more often in battles than on raids. Celtic raiders liked to swoop down on villages and farms in surprise attacks. In battle, the carnyx was used to cause panic among the enemy.

## WAR PAINT

This modern reconstruction shows how a Celtic warrior might have looked as he prepared for a fight. Roman writers reported that the Celts painted or tattooed their bodies with typical Celtic patterns by using woad (a blue dye, made from plants). Today, no one knows what the patterns meant, but Celtic warriors probably believed that they gave them protection, or extra, magic powers.

## RIDING TO RAID

The Celts were expert horse riders, and horses were among their most treasured possessions. These little lead figures were made in south Austria around 650BC. They show Celtic horsemen riding to a raid. Horses were valued almost as highly as humans and were buried respectfully when they died.

## PURE GOLD

These three beautiful gold torcs were made by the Celts in Britain around 50BC. They were worn around the neck by rich men and women. The Celts hoped to seize such treasures when they went on raids. Celtic chieftains shared the captured goods among their followers. They might also give a share as an offering to the gods.

# On Land and Sea

CELTIC IDEAS, technologies and designs spread across a wide area, from the borders of central Asia to the shores of the Atlantic Ocean. Travel in Celtic times was slow and difficult, compared with today. There were no paved roads, although the Celts did build causeways of wood across marshy ground. Overland journeys were made on foot or horseback, and only the wealthiest chiefs could afford to drive in chariots. For carrying heavy loads of farm produce, timber or salt, the Celts used wooden carts pulled by oxen. Celtic boats were built of wood, or of thick leather stretched across a wooden frame. They were powered by men rowing with oars, or by cloth or leather sails which trapped the wind.

It is highly unlikely that any individual traveller would have journeyed from one side of the Celtic lands to the other. However, many Celtic merchants, craftworkers, warriors and raiders made shorter journeys that brought them into contact with neighbouring peoples – both Celts and non-Celts. It seems likely that new ideas and inventions were spread in this way.

### FAST CHARIOT

The early Celts of the Hallstatt era (750–450BC) buried heavy, four-wheeled wagons alongside important people. These wagons were slow and lumbering, useful only for carting heavy loads for short distances, or for ceremonial display. Between about 500BC and 400BC, lighter, faster, two-wheeled chariots, like the one on this coin, became popular in Celtic lands (and in Celtic burials, too). Some chariots were used for war, others were owned as status symbols by rich and powerful rulers.

### FIT FOR A KING
Only the richest Celtic chiefs and warriors could afford to decorate their chariots with fine bronze and enamel fittings, such as this terret ring. It was used as a guide ring through which the horse's reins were passed.

### HEAVY LOAD
This leather rucksack was worn by a Celtic workman about 2,800 years ago. It was found in the Hallstatt salt mines, and was used to carry blocks of rock salt along winding, underground passages that led to the entrance of the mine. This was a common way to carry heavy loads. Only the richest Celts could afford horses and wagons.

## LAKE TRADE

One-person boats, such as this one, had deep, narrow hulls and upturned prows. They were made from planks of wood, and their design was based on the first-ever boats, which were hollowed out logs. They were used to carry cargo (including rock salt) across the Austrian lakes. This little wooden model is 10.5 cm long and was found in Austria.

## SUMMIT PATHS

Long-distance tracks ran along the ridges of lowland hills, such as these chalk downs in southern England. The ground along these hill summits was usually well-drained, so people travelling on foot or on horseback did not sink into the mud. The elegant animal shape cut into this chalk hillside reminds us of the Celts' passion for horses. It may have been made in Celtic times, but some historians think that it is only about 1,000 years old.

## MAGICAL PROTECTION

Wealthy Celtic warriors decorated their horse harnesses (which linked horses to their chariots) with elaborate metal plates. This harness plate would have been placed on the horse's forehead with two others, one on each side of the head. It is ornamented with a typical Celtic three-legged design. The number three was a sign of magic power for the Celts, and the owner of this plate may have hoped it would protect him and his horse from harm.

## SAILING THE SEAS

This beautiful miniature boat, made of solid gold, is about 2,000 years old and was designed as an offering to the gods. It was found in County Derry in Ireland. Like full-sized Celtic boats, it has moveable oars, and a mast for a sail. The slats across the centre were seating for the boat's occupants. Celtic merchants and traders travelled around the coasts of western Europe in boats just like this one.

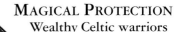

# Weapons and Armour

Celts relied on their strength – and their weapons – to survive in battle. Heavy Celtic swords were made of iron, and were used for cutting and slashing. They were carried in decorated scabbards made of bronze, wood or leather. Spears and javelins were lighter. They were used for stabbing at close quarters, or for throwing at an enemy many metres away. Round pebbles, hurled by cloth or leather slings, could also be deadly weapons. Archaeologists have found huge stockpiles of pebbles at Celtic hill forts. Wooden clubs were used by warriors to bludgeon their enemies in battle, but were also used for hunting birds.

For protection, Celtic warriors carried a long shield, usually made of wood and leather. Normally, Celtic men wore a thigh-length tunic over baggy trousers but, in battle, they often went naked except for a torc (twisted metal ring) around the neck, and a metal helmet. This nakedness was a proud display of physical strength – even the Celts' enemies admired their tall, muscular physique. The Celts believed that torcs gave magical protection. Their helmets, topped with magic crests, gave them extra height and made them look frightening.

## CHAIN MAIL

The Celts sometimes used flexible chest coverings of chain mail in battle. Several burial sites have yielded actual chain mail such as that shown above, found in St Albans, England. However, most of the time, the Celts went into battle naked.

## UNDRESSED TO KILL

This gold pin is decorated with the figure of a naked Celtic warrior, armed with sword, shield and helmet. One ancient writer described a Celtic warrior's weapons: 'A long sword worn on the right side, and a long shield, tall spears, and a kind of javelin. Some also use bows and slings. They have a wooden warclub, which is thrown by hand with a range far greater than an arrow …'

## MAKE A SHIELD

*You will need: felt-tip pen, card 77cm x 38cm, scissors, ruler, pair of compasses, bottle top, bradawl, leather thongs, paper fasteners, sticky tape, drink carton lid, modelling clay, PVA glue, paint, paint-brushes, dowelling 75cm long.*

77 cm
38 cm

**1** Draw a shield shape on to card. The shield should have rounded corners and curve in slightly on each of the long sides, as shown. Cut out.

29 cm
17 cm

**2** Draw a vertical and a horizontal line through the centre of the shield. Add a large circle in the centre and two smaller circles either side, as shown.

**3** With a felt-tip pen draw a typical Celtic design inside the circles, as shown. Use the bottle top and compasses to help you create your design.

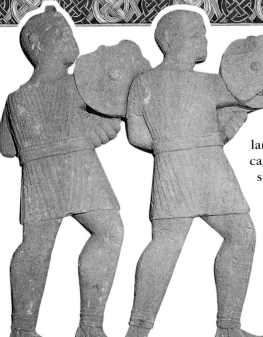

### SPANISH SHIELDS

The design of weapons and armour varied in different Celtic lands. These Celts are carrying small, round shields that originated in Spain. Shields were made from wood and leather. All Spanish warriors usually fought with a short, single-edged sword, called a *falcata*.

### HANDY WEAPON

Daggers were used for fighting at close range. By the end of the Celtic era, when this dagger was made, their strong, sharp blades were usually forged from iron. They often had finely decorated hilts (handles), with scabbards (sheaths) fashioned from softer bronze. This Celtic dagger was found in the River Thames.

### BRAIN GUARD

Helmets were usually made of iron, padded inside with cloth and covered on the outside by a layer of bronze. The high, domed shape protected the wearer's skull, and the peaked front kept slashing sword blows away from the eyes.

### SHARP AND DEADLY

Celtic weapons were fitted with sharp metal blades, designed to cause terrible injuries. This bronze spear-point was made in Britain in about 1400BC, using techniques that were still employed by the Celts a thousand years later. Celtic metalworkers used moulds to make tools and weapons. Molten bronze was poured into the mould. Once the bronze object was cold and hard, rough edges were polished away, using coarse sand.

*Shields were a speciality of craft workshops in southern England. A shield was one of a Celtic warrior's most prized possessions.*

**4** Use the bradawl to make two holes between the large and smaller circles, as shown. Thread the leather thongs through the holes.

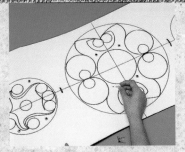

**5** With the bradawl, make small holes for the decorative paper fasteners. Push the paper fasteners through the holes and tape the ends on the back.

**6** Stick the drink carton lid into the centre of the large circle. Roll long, thin clay snakes. Glue them along the lines of your decorative pattern.

**7** Paint the front of the shield bronze. When dry, turn over and stick the dowelling down the back. Use tape to secure. Tie the leather thongs.

# War Against Rome

THE ROMAN PEOPLE lived in southern Italy. At first, they were farmers, but gradually they built up a formidable army and began to conquer the surrounding lands. By the first century AD, they ruled over a vast empire. In order to conquer this empire, the Romans had to fight, especially against the Celts. The first major conflicts began soon after 400BC, when migrating bands of Celts from France arrived in northern Italy. Then, in 387BC, Celtic warriors attacked Rome. For the Romans, the Celts came to represent everything that was savage, barbarian and brutal – a great contrast, the Romans thought, to their own civilized ways of life. They determined to conquer the Celts and take over their lands. It took many years, but they succeeded. Roman soldiers were impressed by the fast, two-horse chariots that Celtic chiefs rode into battle. However, the Romans soon discovered that most of the Celtic troops were no match for their well-organized, disciplined way of fighting, or for their short, stabbing swords. When the Celts saw their hero chiefs dead on the battlefield, the ordinary warriors panicked. They either hurled themselves recklessly towards the Romans, and were easily killed, or else retreated in confusion and despair.

### ROMANS RIDING HIGH
This tombstone was carved as a memorial to a Roman soldier named Flavinus. He served as a standard-bearer in a cavalry regiment that was sent to enforce the Roman conquest of Britain in about AD50. It shows his horse trampling a Celtic warrior under its hoofs. The warrior has hair stiffened with lime to make him look more fierce. Despite their courage, Celtic foot soldiers had little chance of surviving a Roman cavalry charge.

### CAPTIVE CELTS
Once captured by the Romans, Celtic men, women and children were either killed or sold as slaves. This painting dates from the 1800s and shows captive Celts in Rome. The artist has used their imagination to invent some details of the Celts' clothes and hairstyles. After success in war, the Romans paraded captured prisoners through the city.

## TRIUMPH AND DEFEAT

Two Celts, captured and in chains, are depicted on a Roman triumphal arch. The arch was built around AD25 in southern France. It commemorates a Roman victory against the rebellious Gauls. The sculptor has shown the Gauls as the Romans imagined them, looking wild and ragged, and dressed in shaggy fur.

## ENEMIES ON COINS

The Romans chose to show a Celtic warrior in his battle chariot on this Roman coin. They admired certain aspects of the Celtic civilization and were proud to have conquered such a people.

## JULIUS CAESAR

Roman army commander Julius Caesar was very ambitious. He used his success against the Celts in France to help advance his political career in Rome. In 44BC, he declared himself 'Dictator (sole ruler) for Life'. He wrote a book describing his campaigns against the Celts. Although it paints a hostile picture of the Celtic people, Caesar's book has become one of the most important pieces of evidence about Celtic life. This silver coin shows Julius Caesar, represented as an elephant, crushing Gaul (France).

## WALLED FRONTIER

In AD122, the Roman emperor, Hadrian, gave orders for a massive wall to be built across northern England. Its purpose was to mark the border between lands ruled by Rome and lands further north in Scotland, where Celtic chiefs still had power. Roman soldiers were stationed at forts built at intervals along the wall. They kept a look out for Celtic attackers, but also met, traded with, and sometimes married, members of the local Celtic population who lived and worked close to the wall.

# Hilltop Forts

**CLIFFTOP FORTS**
Cliff castles were enclosures made of stone, built at the top of cliffs overlooking the sea. They were designed for defence, as status symbols, and perhaps as lookout points, as well. This 'castle' is at Dun Aengus, on the Aran Islands, off the west coast of Ireland. The stones in the distance were placed around the castle to slow down attackers once they were in range of pebbles and slings.

IN MANY CELTIC LANDS, houses, storerooms and cattle enclosures were surrounded by strong defensive walls. In uncertain times, when there were wars between Celtic tribes, or when Celtic lands were being attacked by outsiders, the Celts built hilltop forts for protection. In Ireland and Brittany, cliff castles were built, and in southern England, Germany and central Europe, there were hill forts. These hilltop forts also served as status symbols, to display the wealth and power of the tribe who built them.

To make a hill fort, teams of workers heaped up huge banks of earth around the summit of a hill, and topped them with strong wooden walls. The raised sites of the forts made it easy for defenders to see enemies advancing, and to hurl deadly spears and pebbles from within the forts' strong walls.

**WHICH WAY TO THE GATE?**
The entrance to the hill fort of Maiden Castle, in southern England, could only be approached through this maze of curved earth banks. The banks were designed to slow down approaching enemies and confuse them. This gave the defenders inside the hill fort a chance to attack their enemies and drive them away. Archaeologists have found the skeletons of many Celtic warriors who died defending Maiden Castle, close to the entrance.

## DEFENCES

The entrance to a hill fort was protected by a strong wooden gate, high ramparts (steep earth banks), and rows of sharp, pointed wooden stakes driven into the ground. Where the land was rocky, as here, the stakes were replaced by rows of sharp stones pointing upwards. Historians call this a *cheveux de frise*, the French words meaning 'frizzy hair'.

## TALL TOWER

In Scotland, Celtic chiefs built massive brochs – tall, round stone towers. Brochs were probably originally safe places for people to shelter in wartime, but they soon became an important way of displaying a tribe's or a chieftain's power. The ruins of many Celtic brochs still survive today. This one is at Mousa, in the Shetland Isles, off the north coast of Scotland.

## SCOTTISH HILL FORT

The hill forts of Dunagoil (left) and Little Dunagoil (centre) were used by the Celts. The ramparts were built of stone with timber-lacing. Following an attack on the fort, the timbers in the ramparts were set alight, causing the stones to heat up and vitrify (turn to glass).

## ALMOST A TOWN

Towards the end of the Celtic era, some hill forts developed into large settlements, almost like towns. This artist's impression shows a typical *oppidum* (defended settlement) in Spain. The streets are laid out in a regular grid pattern, with closely packed blocks of houses. Merchants and craftsmen also had their workshops within the towns.

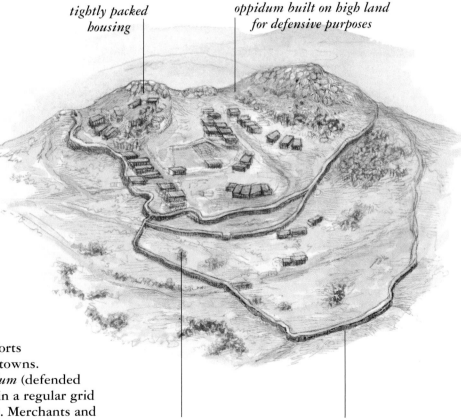

*tightly packed housing*

*oppidum built on high land for defensive purposes*

*lower enclosures*

*surrounded by strong walls*

# Village Homes

**A**LTHOUGH MANY PEOPLE think of the Celts as fierce, wild warriors, most Celtic people were farmers who spent their lives in isolated farmsteads or small villages. The type of settlement depended on when and where it was built. The choice depended on local soils and farming methods, the social customs of the region, ancient traditions, and wartime dangers. Whatever their size, Celtic settlements were usually built close to reliable sources of essential supplies such as water, and fish and animals for hunting. Timber and meadowland for grazing livestock were important too. In addition, natural resources, such as copper and iron ore for smelting metals, clay for pottery making, and fertile soil for growing crops, were also vital.

### FAMILY FARM
In lowland areas of Europe, Celtic families built villages of timber-framed roundhouses. Each family had a large house for living and several smaller buildings for sheltering animals and storing food. Grain was kept in pits underground, to protect it from rats.

### COURTYARD HOMES
This aerial photograph shows the remains of a Celtic village at Chysauster, in Cornwall. It was built between AD1 and AD200. Each family had a house made up of several small stone chambers which were surrounded by circular walls of earth and stone. These walls created a safe courtyard where women could work, children could play, and animals could be sheltered at night. The Celts built their village houses out of locally available materials. For example, in rocky or mountainous regions such as Brittany, Cornwall or Scotland, rough lumps of stone were used to construct buildings.

### MAKE A ROUNDHOUSE
*You will need: string, felt-tip pen, brown card, scissors, ruler, 2 pieces of stiff white card 78cm x 12cm, PVA glue, masking tape, modelling clay, rolling pin, straw, corrugated cardboard, 7 x dowelling 45cm long, bradawl.*

**1** Using the piece of string and a felt-tip pen draw a circle with a radius of 25cm on the stiff brown card. Cut round the circle with the scissors.

**2** Draw notches every 30cm along the edges of the two pieces of white card. Cut in to the notches. Glue the two pieces of card together at one end.

**3** Fit the wall to the base of your house, making sure the notches are along the top. Glue the wall in place and secure it with masking tape.

## BUILDING MATERIALS

Some lowland Celtic houses were rectangular, others were built with circular walls and a conical roof. Both types were constructed around a framework of timber posts. The spaces in-between the wall timbers were filled with woven branches plastered with mud and clay. The roof timbers were covered with a layer of thatch, made from reeds or straw.

*straw*     *timber*

## LAKE VILLAGE

In Scotland, the Celts built small artificial islands, called crannogs, in sheltered lochs (lakes) and rivers. They were connected to the shore by a narrow wooden bridge. Celtic families built their homes here, and surrounded them by wooden walls. They hoped they would be safer than in houses on dry land. This modern reconstruction shows a crannog on Loch Tay in central Scotland.

### AN EXPERIMENT

Archaeologists experiment with different building techniques, such as this reconstructed wattle-and-daub wall, to find out more about how the Celts lived and worked.

## CORACLE TRANSPORT

The Celts made short journeys across rivers and lakes in coracles (boats made of cattle hide stretched across a latticed wooden frame). Coracles were powered and steered with a single paddle. Most had space for only two or three people inside.

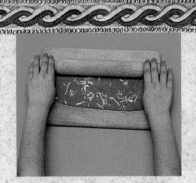

**4** Roll out the modelling clay into long sections 13cm high. Sprinkle straw on to the clay and roll it in. Make enough sections to cover the wall.

**5** Press the clay sections on to the wall until the whole wall is covered. Take care to keep the notches at the top of the wall visible.

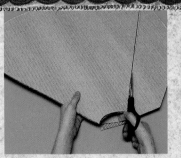

**6** Cut a large circle with a diameter of 91cm from cardboard. Cut a small circle in the centre. Cut the large circle into sections 56cm wide along the outer edge.

**7** Glue straw on to these roof sections, starting on the outside edge and using three layers.

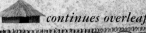 *continues overleaf*

# Inside the Roundhouse

I<small>T WAS DARK AND SMOKY</small> inside a Celtic roundhouse, but quite comfortable. The thatched roof was a good insulator, keeping the house warm in the winter and cool in the summer. Celtic houses were heated by a wood or peat fire burning in a pit in the centre of the room. The hearth was the heart of the home, and the fire was kept burning day and night, all year round. Smoke from the fire drifted upwards, and escaped through the thatch.

There were no smoke-holes. Recently, archaeologists built a replica roundhouse. They found that leaving a hole in the roof to let smoke out led to sudden downdraughts, and risked setting the whole house on fire. Most houses had no windows, the only light coming from the fire or through the open door. The doorways were low, and protected by a tunnel-like porch to keep out wind and rain. The Celts owned little furniture, so people ate and slept on the ground. For warmth and comfort, they covered the pounded earth floor with heaps of animal skins or thick mattresses made of straw.

## BULL BY THE HORNS

As logs burned on the hearth they were held in place by metal props known as firedogs. This is one of a set of four – one stood at each corner of the hearth. The Celts decorated their household goods with patterns and pictures. This iron firedog is topped with a bull's head decoration. The blacksmith has managed to give the bull a lively expression!

## LOCAL LOOK

In different Celtic areas, houses were built to different designs. This Scottish roundhouse has a timber-framed thatched roof – both common local building materials.

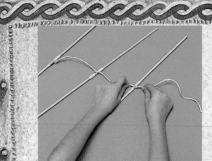

**8** Wrap 2 pieces of masking tape 1cm apart around the middle of 6 dowelling sticks. Tie string between the tape. Allow 13cm of string between each stick.

**9** Take another dowelling stick. Place it in the middle of the base of the house. Secure the stick in an upright position with clay.

**10** Place the sticks for the roof structure over the house. Ask a friend to hold the centre, as shown, while you put sticks into the wall notches.

**11** Use clay to hold the sticks in place in the wall notches. Then tie the top of the sticks securely together with a piece of string.

## FIRES AND FOOD

As well as heating the roundhouse, the fire was also used for cooking. A large metal cauldron was suspended on heavy iron chains from cross beams in the roof. Animal skins, fish and meat could also be hung above the fire. Chemicals in the smoke helped to preserve them, and gave the smoked fish and meat a rich, tangy taste.

*Roundhouses such as this were common in low-lying areas where wood was plentiful.*

**12** Add extra clay around the ends of the sticks and the wall notches. This will help to secure the roof structure firmly in place on the wall.

**13** Tie together the ends of the string between the last two pieces of dowelling. Keep the string taut to stop the sticks from collapsing.

**14** Use the bradawl to make two holes on both edges at the top and bottom of each roof section. Thread a piece of string through each hole.

**15** Use the ends of the string to tie the roof covering firmly on to the roof structure. Do this until the whole of the roof is covered.

# Towns and Trade

Fᴏʀ ᴛʜᴏᴜꜱᴀɴᴅꜱ ᴏꜰ ʏᴇᴀʀꜱ, different parts of Europe have been linked by long-distance trade. Well-known trade routes followed great river valleys, such as the Rhine, the Rhône and the Danube, or connected small ports along the coast, from Ireland to Portugal. As early as 600ʙᴄ, traders from the Mediterranean claimed to have sailed through the Straits of Gibraltar and over the sea to the British Isles. After around 200ʙᴄ, the Celts began to build fortified settlements as centres of government, craftwork and trade. Some grew up around existing hill forts or villages, others occupied fresh sites. The Romans called them *oppida*, the Latin word for town. Some of the oppida were very large. For example, Manching, in southern Germany, covered about 380 hectares, and its protective walls were 7 kilometres long.

### WINE LOVERS
The Celts were very fond of wine, which they imported from Italy. Roman wine merchants transported their wine in tall pottery jars called amphorae. You can see four amphorae at the back of this picture.

### HIGH VALUE
Celts learned how to make coins from the Macedonians, who lived in eastern Europe. The first Celtic coins were made of pure precious metals, such as gold and silver. They were made by stamping a metal disc between two dies (moulds).

### SMALL CHANGE
In the second half of the Celtic era, coins were made from alloys (mixed metals) containing only a small amount of silver or gold. These coins were much less valuable than the earlier, pure metal ones. This alloy coin was made around 100ʙᴄ in western France.

### MAKE A WAGON
*You will need: white card, ruler, felt-tip pen, scissors, balsa wood, PVA glue, masking tape, sandpaper, pair of compasses, paint and paintbrush, drawing pins, bradawl, leather thong.*

**1** Take a piece of stiff white card measuring 29cm x 16cm. Using a ruler and felt-tip pen, draw lines 2cm in from the edges of the card.

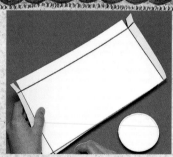

**2** Make cuts in the corners of the card, as shown. Score along the lines and fold the edges up to make a box shape. This is the body of the wagon.

**3** Take a piece of card 27cm x 12cm. Take two lengths of balsa wood 20cm long. Stick them across the card, 4cm in from the two ends.

KEY
- ⚲ Iron
- ⚭ Tin
- ⚱ Amphorae (wine jars)
- ⚯ Amber
- ⚰ Salt

GREAT BRITAIN
MAITHABY
KEMMELBERG
UXISAME
MOSOMAGUS
STEINSBURG
LUTETIA
CONTIOMAGUS
RUBIN
MELUN
HERAPE
SEGODUNUM
ZAVIST
CENABUM
REINHEIM
MT LASSOIS
HEUNEBERG
STUPAVA
CHASSEY
ROANNE
CHATILLON-SUR-GLANE
LUGDUNUM
MANTUA
ESTE
SPINA
CELTIBERIA
(SPAIN AND PORTUGAL)
MASSALIA
FELSINA

## LONG-DISTANCE TRADE

Celtic merchants and craftworkers in different lands were linked together by a network of trade routes, leading north-south and east-west. Few traders would have travelled the length of any one route. Instead, merchants from different countries met at trading towns. Valuable goods might be bought and sold several times along a trade route before reaching their final owner.

## TOWN WALLS

Oppida were surrounded by strong, defensive walls. These ruined ones are from a Celtic town in southern France. Within the walls, houses, streets and craft workshops were laid out in well-planned, orderly rows.

*This model wagon is based on the remains of funeral wagons found buried in Celtic graves. The Celts used wagons that were more roughly made but easier to steer for carrying heavy loads.*

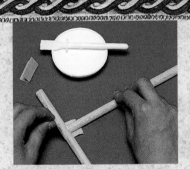

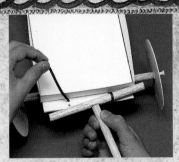

**4** Take two sticks of balsa wood 26cm and 11cm long. Sand the end of the long stick to create a slight indent to fit against the short piece. Glue together.

**5** Use the pair of compasses to draw four circles, each 10cm in diameter, out of card. Next, carefully cut the circles out, as shown above.

**6** Glue the box on to the piece of card. Attach the wheels to the balsa wood shafts by pressing a drawing pin through the centre of each wheel.

**7** Make two holes in the front of the wagon with a bradawl. Thread the leather thong through the holes and attach the steering pole. Paint the wagon silver.

# Fields and Animals

THE CELTS WERE FARMING PEOPLE. They cleared fields, planted crops, and bred livestock. They also fenced meadowland, and kept out their grazing animals until they had cut and dried the meadow grass to make hay for winter fodder. Celtic farmers used an iron-tipped plough, pulled by oxen, to turn over the soil in their fields and prepare the ground for planting. Seeds of grain were scattered by hand on ploughed land in early spring; the crops were ready to harvest in late summer or autumn. The Celts' most important crops were wheat, oats and barley, which could be cooked to make porridge, or ground into flour.

The most common farm animals were pigs, cattle, sheep and goats. As well as producing meat, animals provided milk (used to make butter and cheese), wool (spun and woven into cloth), and hides (which were tanned to make leather). The Celts also reared ducks and geese, for meat and eggs. Manure from animals and birds was used as a fertilizer on the fields. In some areas, Celtic farmers dug pits for marl (natural lime) to spread on their land. The lime helped to fertilize the soil and make the crops grow.

**BULL'S EYE**
Cattle were the most important farm animals in many Celtic lands. Oxen were used to pull carts and farm machinery, as well as for food. All cattle were highly prized, and were the main source of wealth for many farmers. Irish myths and legends tell of daring raids, when Celtic warriors galloped off to attack enemy farms and take all their cattle away.

**SICKLE AND HOE**
As crops grew in the fields, the Celtic farmer used a hoe (right) to keep the weeds down. The crops were harvested with a sharp, curved sickle (above). This hoe and sickle date from the La Tène era (450–50BC). Farming tools such as these were made by blacksmiths out of iron. Grain crops and hay were sometimes cut by an animal-drawn reaping machine, called a *vallus*. It was made of wood, with iron cutting blades.

**PAIR OF PIGS**
The Celts raised pigs on their farms as well as hunting wild boar in the woods. Farm pigs were much smaller and thinner than European pigs today. They had long legs and stripy, bristly hair. In Celtic art, the boar was a symbol of great strength and power. These two little bronze pigs were probably made as offerings to the gods.

## RARE BREED
The Soay sheep is an ancient breed that is rare today. It is similar to the sheep kept by Celtic farmers. It is small, nimble and hardy, and has long horns. Soay sheep do not need shearing because their fleece sheds naturally in summer. The wool can then be combed or pulled out by hand.

## GRACEFUL GOOSE
This stone slab was carved in Scotland, in about AD450. It shows a goose turning round to preen its tail feathers. Geese were kept for their meat, eggs and grease. Goose grease could be rubbed on sore, dry skin, and used to soften and waterproof leather. Although the evidence has not survived, it seems likely that soft goose feathers were used to make warm bedding as well.

## GOOD GRAINS
The Celts' main food crops were grains such as wheat, barley, oats and rye. These crops were harvested in late summer, heated over firepits to remove moisture, then stored in underground chambers (historians call them souterrains) for winter use.

*wheat*

*barley*

## RIDGE AND FURROW
This photo shows ancient ridges and furrows in south-west England, created by later medieval farmers using techniques that may have been developed by the Celts. During the Celtic era, farmers began to move away from the light, well-drained soils on hilltops and slopes, clearing new fields on the heavier, wetter but more fertile land in valley bottoms. They invented heavy ploughs, fitted with wheels and pulled by oxen, to help cultivate this land.

# Life on the Farm

**M**EN, WOMEN AND CHILDREN were all expected to play their parts in running a Celtic farm. It seems likely that both men and women worked in the fields. Men usually did the ploughing, but the women probably carried out tasks such as weeding the crops. Everyone helped at harvest time because it was vital to gather the grain as soon as it was ripe. There were countless other jobs that needed doing to keep the farm running smoothly, such as combing sheep, caring for sick animals, milking cows, collecting eggs, repairing thatched roofs, and fetching water. Along with all the other tasks around the farm, parents had to teach their children the skills they would need in adult life. Many Celtic parents sent their sons and daughters to live in other households until they were grown up. This was a way of making close bonds of friendship between families and tribes and also taught the children extra skills.

### WRAPPED AND WARM
This carved stone statue of a baby wrapped in a blanket was made in Celtic France. Compared with today, it must have been difficult for mothers and grandmothers to keep young children clean, warm, dry and out of danger on a busy farm.

### LOCKED UP
Keys like these were used to lock wooden chests containing valuable goods, such as the family's marriage wealth. This was the bride's dowry (money or treasure given by her father) plus an equal amount given by the husband on their wedding day. In some Celtic lands, wives had the right to inherit this if they outlived their husbands.

### MAKE A POT
*You will need: paper, bowl, PVA glue, water, balloon, petroleum jelly, card, pair of compasses, pencil, ruler, scissors, masking tape, cardboard core from roll of adhesive tape, pin, red and black paint, paintbrushes.*

**1** To make papier-mâché, tear paper or newspaper up into small strips. Fill a bowl with 1 part PVA glue to 3 parts water. Add the paper pieces and soak.

**2** Blow up the balloon and cover in petroleum jelly. Cover the balloon in a layer of papier-mâché mixture. Leave to dry, then slowly build up more layers.

**3** On the card draw a circle 20cm in diameter. Draw a second circle inside it 9cm in diameter. Mark off a quarter of both circles. Cut the large circle out.

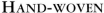

## DYED IN THE WOOL

The Romans reported that the Celts liked patterned, brightly coloured clothes. Sheep's wool was often dyed before being woven into cloth. Dyes were made from flowers, bark, berries, leaves or lichen boiled together with salt, crushed rock or stale urine. The wool was soaked in this mixture then boiled again, or left to soak for several hours.

*sheep's wool*     *lichen*

## HAND-WOVEN

Many Celtic women made clothes and blankets from sheep's wool from their own farms. First, they cleaned and sorted the wool, then they spun it into thread. The thread was woven on an upright loom. Heavy weights kept the warp (vertical) threads straight while the weft (horizontal) thread was passed in-between.

## PEDESTAL POTS

Celtic women made simple pottery bowls and dishes for use at home. Wealthy Celtic people could also afford elegant vases and jugs like these pedestal pots (pots with feet), made by expert craftworkers in towns.

## BUTTER BUCKET

Wooden buckets such as this were used on many Celtic farms, but few have survived. This one was found buried in a bog in northern Scotland. It contained butter. The damp, airless conditions in the bog had stopped the wood rotting.

*Decorate your pedestal pot with a swirling pattern in typical Celtic style. The Celts liked bright colours – the pot that inspired this model was originally bright red.*

**4** Cut out a quarter of the outer circle and all of the inner circle, as shown. The outer circle will be the pot base. Stick the ends together with tape.

**5** Use the cardboard inner from a roll of adhesive tape to make the stem of the pot. Attach it to the card base with masking tape.

**6** Burst the balloon with a pin. Cut the top end of the pot off evenly. Attach the base and stem to the bottom of the pot with masking tape.

**7** Paint the whole pot with red paint, including the stem and neck. Then add the Celtic pattern, as shown above, in black paint.

# Food and Drink

Food was very important to the Celts. They enjoyed eating and drinking, and were not ashamed of getting drunk, or of rowdy behaviour. They did not, however, approve of people getting too fat. Roman writers reported that Celtic warriors were ordered not to let out their belts, but to lose weight, when clothes around their waists became too tight! The Celts produced most of their own food on their farms. They needed to buy only items such as salt (used to preserve meat and fish), and luxury goods such as wine. They also hunted and fished for many wild creatures, and gathered wild fruits, nuts, herbs and mushrooms from meadows and forests. Celtic families were famous throughout Europe for their hospitality to strangers. It was their custom to offer food and drink to any visitor, and not to ask who they were or where they were from until the end of the meal.

### Hanging Cauldron
Meals for large numbers of people were cooked in a big cauldron. This bronze cauldron, iron chain and hook were made around 300BC in Switzerland. A cauldron could also be used for boiling water, heating milk to make cheese, or brewing mead.

### Celtic Casserole
Meat, beans, grains and herbs were stewed in a covered clay pot. The pot could be placed directly on glowing embers or (as shown here) balanced on a hearthstone. This stone hearth, with a hollow pit for the fire, was found at an oppidum (Celtic town) in France.

## Make some Oatcakes

*You will need: 225g oatmeal, 75g plain flour, salt, baking soda, 50g butter, water, bowl, sieve, wooden spoon, small saucepan, heat-resistant glass, board, rolling pin, baking tray, wire tray.*

1 Preheat the oven to 220°C/425°F/Gas 7. Put 225g of oatmeal into a large bowl. Add 75g of plain flour. Sieve the flour into the bowl.

2 Next add 1 teaspoon of salt to the oatmeal and flour mixture. Mix all the ingredients in the bowl together well using a wooden spoon.

3 Add a quarter teaspoon of bicarbonate of soda (baking soda) to the oatmeal and flour mixture. Mix it in well and then put the bowl to one side.

## GRINDING GRAIN

All kinds of grain were ground into flour using hand-powered querns (mills) like this one. The grains were poured through a hole in the top stone. This stone was then turned round and round. The grains became trapped and were crushed between the top and bottom stones, spilling out of the quern sides as flour.

## FRUITS FROM THE FOREST

The Celts liked eating many of the same fruits and nuts that we enjoy today. However, they had to go and find them growing on bushes and trees. We know that the Celts ate fruit because archaeologists have found many seeds and pips on rubbish heaps and in lavatory pits at Celtic sites.

*wild cherries*

*apples*

*hazelnuts*

*blackberries*

## OUT HUNTING

Celtic men went hunting and fishing for sport, and also as a way of finding food. This stone carving, showing a huntsman and his dogs chasing deer, was made around AD800 in Scotland. By then, Celtic power had declined, but many Celtic traditions persisted.

*Enjoy your oatcakes plain, like the Celts did, or eat them with butter, cheese or honey. All these were favourite Celtic foods. Today, some people put jam on their oatcakes, but sugar (used to make jam) was unknown in Europe in Celtic times.*

**4** Next, melt the butter in a small saucepan over a low heat. Make sure that it does not burn. Add the melted fat to the oat and flour mixture.

**5** Boil some water. Place a little of the water in a mug or heat-resistant glass. Gradually add the boiled water to the mixture until you have a firm dough.

**6** Turn the dough out on to a board sprinkled with a little oatmeal and flour. Roll the dough until it is about 1cm thick. Cut the dough into 24 circles.

**7** Place the circles of dough on a greased baking tray. Bake in the oven for 15 minutes. Allow the oatcakes to cool on a wire tray before serving.

# A Celtic Feast

CELTIC STORIES AND POEMS often describe splendid feasts, in which food is served all day and all night. These feasts were far more than occasions for eating and drinking. They were a way of bonding together all the most important men in a community, of displaying wealth and power, of settling quarrels between warriors, and of deciding status within the tribe. Feasts were for men only, although women often cooked and served the food. The host and his guests, warrior heroes or noblemen, sat in a circle, with the honoured guest (usually the bravest hero) in the seat of honour. The assembled company might be entertained by a musician, who composed songs in their praise. The honoured guest was served with the choicest cut of meat (from the thigh), called the champion's portion. But if another guest felt he was braver, then he would claim the portion, and the two would fight.

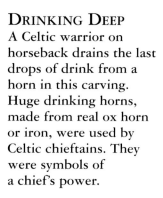

**DRINKING DEEP**
A Celtic warrior on horseback drains the last drops of drink from a horn in this carving. Huge drinking horns, made from real ox horn or iron, were used by Celtic chieftains. They were symbols of a chief's power.

**WINE CUP**
At a feast, wine and mead were served in huge buckets or bowls then poured into individual cups. This bronze cup was made in the British Isles in about AD40. Its handle is shaped like a waterbird.

## PLAY THE GAME

*You will need: modelling clay, rolling pin, wooden board, ruler, clay cutting tool or pencil, paint and paintbrushes.*

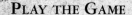

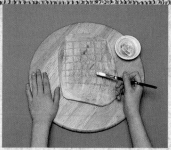

1 Roll out the clay using the board and rolling pin. The finished slab should measure about 20cm x 15cm, and be about 1.5cm thick.

2 Using a cutting tool, mark out a grid. It should have seven horizontal and seven vertical lines. Make a small circular pit in the centre with a pencil.

3 Leave the board in a warm place to dry. Cover the slab with dilute grey paint, as shown. Then leave the board in a warm place to dry.

### IRON BLADES

The Celts ate with knives, spoons or their fingers, as forks were not invented until the Middle Ages. These iron meat-cutting knives were made in Germany in about AD50. Their blades are similar in shape to many cooking knives today. For comfort, their handles might have been bound with string (woven from plant fibres) or leather thongs.

### MEAD AND ALE

The Celts brewed two of their favourite alcoholic drinks at home, using local ingredients. Mead was made from honey and herbs, and ale was made from barley and flavoured with heather. Grapes for making wine did not grow well in many Celtic lands, so wine was imported.

*grapes*

*honey*

*heather*

### GAMING PIECES

The Celts enjoyed playing games and making bets. These little glass counters were made by Celtic craftworkers and were used for gambling, or playing board games.

### BUCKET FOR BANQUETS

This finely decorated bronze bucket was made in about 100BC. It was probably used for mixing wine with water before offering it to guests. In wine-growing countries, wine was always diluted with water, so that guests would not get too drunk!

*No one knows exactly what board games the Celts played. You could use your counters to play draughts, or invent a game of your own.*

**4** Using your fingertips and palms, mould counters, as shown. The counters should have flat bottoms. Make 12 counters.

**5** Divide the counters into threes. Paint the counters in the first group with the same swirly design. Choose a different combination of colours for each group.

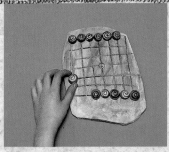

**6** Now combine the pieces to make two separate sets with different patterns. Place the counters at either end of the grid, as shown.

**7** The Celts probably played on the intersections rather than the squares. The central circle may have been a safe haven where the pieces cannot be taken.

# Celtic Clothes

THE CELTS LOVED FINE CLOTHES AND RICH JEWELS. The Greek geographer, Strabo, wrote about the appearance of the Celts: 'They wear gold jewellery, torcs on their necks, and bracelets on their arms and wrists, while people of high rank wear dyed garments ornamented with gold.' Celtic women's clothes were long and loose. Depending on the season, they might be light linen, or thick, warm wool, but the style was usually the same – a sleeveless tunic over a long dress, with a lightweight shift (a simple undergarment) beneath. Over these clothes, women wore a shawl or a cloak that fastened at the shoulder.

At this time, most men wore tunics, but Celtic men were unusual because they wore trousers. This was a style they had copied from nomads from beyond the eastern borders of Europe. Like the Celts, the nomads were keen horse riders, and the Celts found that trousers were more practical for riding than tunics. They were also much warmer in winter. Over their trousers, Celtic men wore a short tunic and a cloak. Jewellery was similar for both women and men. Only wealthy people could afford gold, but ordinary people still liked to wear bracelets and necklaces of cheaper metals, such as bronze, and polished stone or pottery beads. Chiefs often rewarded their best warriors with rich gifts of fine gold arm-rings.

### FLOWING ROBES
This Roman statue shows a Celtic woman from northern Italy during a battle. She is dressed in a knee-length tunic worn over a long, full-skirted dress. Over her left arm she has draped a cloak or shawl, and there is a wide, leather belt around her waist. She is also wearing a bracelet around her right wrist.

### CELTIC CHECKS
The Celts were fond of bright colours and checked patterns. This fragment of brown and green check cloth (lying on top of a modern reconstruction) is one of the oldest pieces of fabric in the world. It was made from hand-spun wool and coloured with plant dyes. The cloth was found in the Hallstatt salt mines, and was made about 2,800 years ago. Spinning, dyeing and weaving cloth was women's work.

## FOR WINTER WEATHER

A Celtic craftworker designed this hooded cape to keep the wearer warm in winter time. It is woven from wool, and has a band of decorative weaving and a long, tasselled fringe around its lower edge. It was made in the Orkney Islands, off the north coast of Scotland, between about AD250 and AD600.

## SALTED SHOES

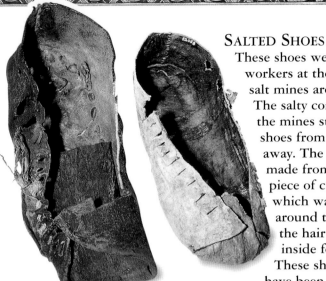

These shoes were worn by workers at the Hallstatt salt mines around 500BC. The salty conditions in the mines stopped the shoes from rotting away. The shoes are made from a single piece of calf-skin which was wrapped around the foot with the hair on the inside for warmth. These shoes would have been held in place by long laces, rather like those used in modern trainers.

## TUNIC AND TROUSERS

This Celtic musician from Spain is comfortably dressed in tunic, trousers and short cloak. He is wearing shoes similar to the ones shown in the picture above. His short, thick hair is brushed back from the forehead in a favourite Celtic style. Few Celtic men let their hair grow very long, but cut it off about level with the bottom of their ears.

## PRETTY WOMAN

The beautiful princess Etain is depicted in this painting from the 1800s. She was described in ancient Irish legends as the most beautiful woman in the world. These descriptions give us some clues of the Celts' ideas about beauty. According to the legends, Etain had bright eyes, like flowers, dark eyebrows, like a beetle's wing, and white teeth, like pearls. Her long hair was plaited into braids, and her cheeks were pink, like foxgloves.

# Proud and Beautiful

Celtic men and women took great pride in their appearance because it made people admire them – and it could be useful. The Romans reported that different groups of men within Celtic society cut their hair and shaved their faces in different styles. This made it clear how important they were. Legends told that warriors who did not have blonde hair (preferred by the Celts) sometimes bleached their hair with a mixture of urine and wood-ash. Before a battle, they might also make their hair stand up on their heads like a crest, using a similar mixture. They hoped this would scare their enemies. Looking good could also work magic. The Celts wore gold torcs because they had special protective powers. For the same reason they sometimes painted or tattooed their bodies with a dark blue dye, called woad.

### A Chieftain's Moustache
This stone carving of a Celtic chieftain was made around 100BC in the Czech Republic. Celtic chieftains shaved their beards but grew long, drooping moustaches. Like the torc this chieftain is wearing around his neck, moustaches were a sign of high status.

### Polished Mirror
Mirrors made of polished metal were among Celtic women's most treasured possessions. Craftworkers in Britain became especially skilled at making them between around 100BC and AD100. This mirror is made of bronze. The back is covered with a swirling design and the handle is carefully shaped to match.

### Make a Brooch
*You will need: rolling pin, modelling clay, board, clay tool, pencil, sandpaper, paints, paintbrush, safety pin, sticky tape.*

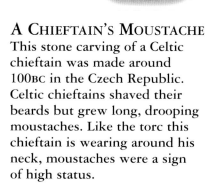

1 Roll out the modelling clay on a board to about 15cm x 15cm. Copy a dragon shape on to the clay, using the finished brooch on the next page as a guide.

2 Cut the brooch shape out of the clay. With the modelling tool, start to draw some of the detail, as shown, into the centre of your brooch.

3 Cut the interior hole out of the brooch. Next add the dragon's two faces and more decorative patterns using a modelling tool, as shown.

## ADORNMENT AND CLEANLINESS

The Celts made several different beauty preparations from natural materials. They mixed stale urine and wood-ash to make a kind of soap. Slaked lime (made by burning crushed limestone) was also mixed with water to bleach and stiffen their hair. They also made a deep blue dye to paint patterns on their skin, from woad, a plant related to flax.

*woad*

*soap*

*lime*

## ALMOST A RING

The shape of this type of brooch is known as penannular (almost a ring). They were worn on the shoulder to keep heavy cloaks in place. This brooch is made of silver and gold, and is studded with pieces of glass and amber.

## HEAVY TO WEAR

Large bronze rings, similar to this one, have been found around the ankles of skeletons in Celtic graves. They must have been heavy to wear, but looking good was more important than comfort!

## BRAIDED HAIR

This gold and silver head of a goddess appears on one of the most famous Celtic objects – the Gundestrup Bowl. The bowl was made in eastern Europe in around 50BC. The artist has shown a tiny human serving-woman plaiting the goddess's hair in a popular Celtic style.

*The brooch that inspired this design was made in Britain in around AD100. Brooches like this one are sometimes called dragon brooches.*

**4** Finish the patterns on your brooch with the sharp end of a pencil. Leave the brooch in a warm place, such as an airing cupboard, to dry.

**5** Next, gently hold the brooch in one hand. With your other hand, sand the edges carefully until they are almost completely smooth.

**6** Paint the brooch with a light blue background colour. Add dark blue and white decorations. Put the brooch to one side until it is completely dry.

**7** Stick the safety pin on to the back of your brooch with a small piece of sticky tape, as shown. Pin the brooch on your T-shirt or top.

# Metalworking

METALWORKERS WERE SOME of the most important people in Celtic society. They made many of the items that Celtic people valued most, from bronze and iron swords to beautiful gold jewellery. It took several years to learn all the necessary skills, first to produce metal from raw nuggets or lumps of ore, and then to shape it. Metalworkers probably began their training very young, but even skilled workers seemed to have been ready to learn. Patterns and techniques invented in one part of the Celtic world were quickly copied and spread to other parts. Celtic metalworkers excelled in several different techniques. Heavy objects were cast from solid bronze, using a clay mould. Iron was heated in a very hot fire to soften it, then hammered into shape. Thin sheets of silver and bronze were decorated with repoussé (pushed out) designs. The designs were sketched on to the back of the metal, then gently hammered to create raised patterns.

### PROTECTION FOR THE HAND

This bronze shieldboss was made in southern Britain between about 200BC and 10BC. A boss is the metal plate that was fixed to the centre of a shield to protect the hand of the person holding it. This example is decorated with a raised pattern of leaves and bird heads, using the repoussé technique.

### TOOLS OF THE TRADE

Many bronze items, such as this horse's bit (below) and harness-ring (far left), were made by pouring molten metal into clay moulds, then leaving it to cool and become solid. You can also see fragments of the clay moulds, and the little crucible used for melting the bronze (top left).

### MAKE A MIRROR

*You will need: pair of compasses, pencil, ruler, stiff gold mirror card, scissors, tracing paper, pen, modelling clay, board, gold paint, paintbrush, PVA glue.*

1 With the compasses, draw a circle 22cm wide on to gold card. Cut out. Use this circle as a template to draw a second circle on to gold card.

2 Cut out the second gold circle. Draw another circle on tracing paper. Fold the piece of tracing paper in two and draw a Celtic pattern in pencil.

3 Lay the tracing paper on to one of the circles. Trace the pattern on to half of the gold circle, then turn the paper over and repeat. Go over the pattern with a pen.

## FROM EARTH AND SEA

The most valuable materials for metalworking were difficult and sometimes dangerous to find. Silver ore was dug from mines underground, or from veins in rocks on the surface. Miners searched for nuggets of gold in gravel at the bottom of fast-flowing streams. Swimmers and divers hunted for coral that grew on little reefs in the Mediterranean Sea.

*bronze ore*

*coral*

*gold nuggets*

## BANDS OF GOLD

The Celts of the Hallstatt era (750–450BC) liked to wear bold, dramatic jewellery, such as the armband and ankle rings shown here. They were found in a tomb in central France. Both the armband and the ankle rings were made of sheets of pure gold and twisted gold wire which were carefully hammered and soldered together.

## DELICATE DESIGN

This clothing toggle was created using the lost wax method of casting. The shape of the piece was modelled in beeswax, then the fine details were added. The wax model was covered with a thick layer of clay. Then the clay-covered model was heated, and the wax ran out. Finally, molten gold was poured into the space where the wax had been.

## TOOLS OF THE TRADE

These little bone spatulas (knives for scooping and spreading) were used by metalworkers to add fine details to the surface of wax models when casting bronze objects using the lost wax process.

*The bronze on a Celtic mirror would have polished up so that the owner could see his or her reflection in it.*

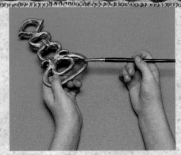

**4** Roll out several snakes of modelling clay and sculpt them into a handle, as shown here. The handle should be about 15cm long and 9cm wide.

**5** Leave the modelling clay to dry. Then paint one side of the handle with gold paint. Leave to dry, then turn over and paint the other side.

**6** Stick the two pieces of mirror card together, white side to white side. Glue the handle on to one side of the mirror.

# Arts and Crafts

ART WAS ESSENTIAL to the Celts. Beautiful objects were not only good to look at, they also carried important messages about their owner's wealth and power. Their designs might have a magic or religious meaning to protect people from harm, or to inspire warriors setting off to war. The Celts were skilled at many different arts and crafts. Many examples of their pottery, glass, enamel, metalwork and jewellery remain for us to admire. From written descriptions of their clothes, we also know that the Celts were skilled weavers and dyers, although few pieces of cloth have survived.

We do not know much about the people who made these fine objects. They may have been free and independent, or the skilled slaves of wealthy families. However, from the archaeological evidence that survives we do know that, towards the end of the Celtic period, many Celtic craftworkers worked in oppida (fortified towns) instead of in country villages, as before.

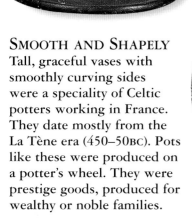

**SMOOTH AND SHAPELY**
Tall, graceful vases with smoothly curving sides were a speciality of Celtic potters working in France. They date mostly from the La Tène era (450–50BC). Pots like these were produced on a potter's wheel. They were prestige goods, produced for wealthy or noble families.

**ANGULAR ART**
During the Hallstatt era (750–450BC), Celtic potters decorated their wares with spiky, angular designs like the patterns on this pottery dish. After about 500BC, when compasses were introduced into Celtic lands from countries near the Mediterranean Sea, designs based on curves and circles began to replace patterns made up of angles and straight lines.

---

## MAKE A TORC

*You will need: board, modelling clay, ruler, string, scissors, PVA glue and brush, gold or bronze paint, paintbrush.*

**1** On the board, roll out two lengths of modelling clay, as shown. Each length should be approximately 60cm long and about 1cm thick.

**2** Keeping the two lengths of clay on the board, plait them together. Leave about 5cm of the clay unplaited at either end, as shown.

**3** Make loops out of the free ends by joining them together. Dampen the ends with a little water to help join the clay if necessary.

## PRECIOUS BOX

This gold and silver box is associated with St Columba. It was made in Scotland and was designed to hold Christian holy relics. After the saint's death, it was kept as a lucky talisman, and carried into battle by Scottish armies. They believed that St Columba would bring them victory.

## GLASS JEWELS

The Celts used glass in different ways to create beautiful objects. Glass was made from salt, crushed limestone and sand, and coloured by adding powdered minerals. Craftworkers melted and twisted different coloured strands together to make jewel-like beads. Glass was also used as enamel, a thin, transparent layer bonded to metal underneath.

*manganese*

*glass*

*cobalt*

*lead*

## MAKING WAVES

The sides of this pot are decorated with a moulded pattern of overlapping waves. The pot has survived unbroken from the La Tène era over 2,000 years ago. It was found in France and it is made from fired clay. Celtic potters built elaborate kilns to fire (bake) their pots at high temperatures.

## ELEGANT ENAMEL

This bronze plaque is decorated with red and yellow enamel. It was made in southern Britain around 50BC and was designed to be worn on a horse's harness.

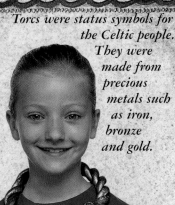

*Torcs were status symbols for the Celtic people. They were made from precious metals such as iron, bronze and gold.*

**4** With the ruler, measure an opening between the two looped ends. The ends should be about 9cm apart so that the torc fits easily around your neck.

**5** When the torc is semi-dry, cut two pieces of string about 8cm long. Use the string to decorate the torc's looped ends. Glue the string in place.

**6** Allow the clay to dry completely. When it is hard, cover all the clay and string with gold or bronze paint. Leave to dry.

# Messages in Stone

THERE WERE SEVERAL DIFFERENT Celtic languages, but no Celtic alphabet. To write something down, the Celts had to borrow other peoples' scripts. Sometimes they used Greek letters, sometimes Latin (the Romans' language). In the British Isles, a script known as Ogham was based on the Latin alphabet, but used straight lines instead of letters. Celtic craftworkers used all these different ways of writing to carve messages in stone. Their inscriptions might commemorate an important event, or a person who had died, or be a proud symbol of a leader's power. Craftworkers also decorated stones with beautiful patterns, sometimes copied from jewellery and metalworking designs. In some parts of the Celtic world, standing stones and lumps of rock were carved with special symbols. Historians think that these picture-carvings were designed to increase respect for powerful leaders, and for the gods.

### STANDING STONE
Tall, carved standing stones were a special feature of Celtic lands in north-west France and Ireland. Archaeologists are not sure why they were put up or decorated, but they probably marked boundaries or holy sites. This stone comes from Turoe, in Ireland.

### PRACTICE MAKES PERFECT
Before using precious metals such as gold, or starting to chip away at hard, valuable materials such as stone, craftworkers made sketches and worked out patterns on little pieces of bone. These bone fragments, marked with compass designs, were found in Ireland. They belonged to craftworkers from around AD50.

### MAKE AN OGHAM STONE

*You will need: modelling clay, board, rolling pin, ruler, modelling tool, sandpaper, white paint, paintbrush, green card, scissors, PVA glue.*

1 Roll out the modelling clay to make a strip roughly 33cm long, 5cm wide and 3cm thick. Carefully shape the top as shown.

2 Take the modelling tool and make a hole in the top end of the strip. This tall 'holed' Ogham stone is based on one in southern Ireland from AD400.

3 These are some of the Ogham letters.

## ON LIVING ROCK

This rough slab of stone is decorated with a Pictish carving of a wild boar. It was found in Dunadd, Scotland. Archaeologists have many theories as to why it was carved. It may have been a memorial to a dead leader or a notice announcing an alliance between friendly clans. An alternative view is that it was a tribal symbol, put up as a proud boast of the local peoples' power or a sign of a local chieftain's land.

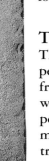

## THE CELTS LIVE ON

The Picts were a mysterious people who lived in Scotland from about AD300 to 900. They were descended from Celtic people and they continued many of the Celts' customs and traditions. In particular, they carved picture-symbols and Ogham letters on stone slabs, in caves and on lumps of rock. This stone monument, from Orkney, Scotland, shows three warriors and various other common Pictish symbols.

## ALL CHANGE

Many tall, carved stones had religious power for the Celts. When Christian missionaries arrived in Celtic lands, they sometimes decided to make old carved stones into Christian monuments. They hoped this might help people understand that the Christian God was more important than the old Celtic ones. This stone is at Oronsay in the Orkney Islands off the north-east coast of Scotland.

*Ogham is sometimes referred to as the 'tree alphabet' because each letter takes the name of a tree. In many cases the Ogham inscription on a stone is read from the bottom up and contains the name of the person being commemorated and that of the carver.*

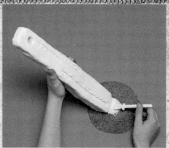

**4** Ogham writing is done as a series of lines or notches scored across a long stem. Use the alphabet in step 3 to help you write something on your stone.

**5** Ogham inscriptions are often found on memorials featuring a person's name. You could try writing your name on your model Ogham stone.

**6** Sand the modelling clay gently to remove any rough edges. Then paint one side of your stone. Leave to dry, turn over and paint the other side.

**7** Cut a circular base out of green card, roughly 14cm wide. Glue the bottom of your stone on to the base, as shown. Now leave the stone to dry.

# Bards and Musicians

THE CELTS ENJOYED MUSIC, poems and songs as entertainment, and for more serious purposes. Music accompanied Celtic warriors into battle and made them feel brave. Poems praised the achievements of a great chieftain or the adventures of bold raiders, and recorded the history of a tribe. Dead chieftains and heroes, and possibly even ordinary people, too, were mourned with sad laments. On special occasions, and in the homes of high-ranking Celts, poems and songs were performed by people called bards. Roman writers described the many years of training to become a bard. Bards learned how to compose using all the different styles of poetry, and memorised hundreds of legends and songs. They also learned how to play an instrument, and to read and write, although most Celtic music and poetry was never written down. Becoming a bard was the first step towards being a druid (priest).

## HOLY MUSIC

We do not know what part music played in Celtic religious ceremonies, but it was probably important. This stone statue shows a Celtic god playing a lyre. The Celts believed that religious knowledge, and music, was too holy to be written down. Sadly, this means that many Celtic poems and songs have been lost for ever.

## GRACEFUL DANCER

Naked dancing girls may have entertained guests at important feasts. This little bronze statue, just 13cm high, dates from around 50BC. The Celts enjoyed dancing, and from the evidence of this statue it seems likely that their dances were quite wild in their movements.

## MAKE A HARP

*You will need: card 39cm x 49cm, pencil, ruler, scissors, cardboard 39cm x 49cm , felt-tip pen, paints, paintbrushes, bradawl, coloured string, paper fasteners.*

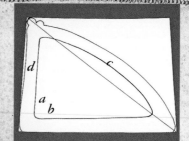

1 On the piece of card, draw a diagonal line from corner to corner. Draw a second, gently curving line, shaped at one end, as shown.

2 Draw two lines (*a* and *b*) 4.5cm in from the edge of the paper. Join them with a curved line *c*. Finally add a curved line *d* parallel to *a*, as shown.

3 Cut out the harp shape. Place it on cardboard. Carefully draw round it with a felt-tip pen both inside and out. Cut the cardboard harp out.

## HARPIST

This harpist is pictured on the Dupplin Cross, from Scotland. The harp itself is large and triangular in shape. It was placed on the ground and held between the harpist's knees. Such harps were popular at the end of the Celtic period.

## MUSICAL GROUP

Musicians are shown playing at a religious ceremony on this stone carving from Scotland, dating from around AD900. The bottom panel shows a harpist plucking the strings of his harp, while a fellow musician plays a pipe. In the foreground is a drum, possibly made from a barrel with a skin stretched over it.

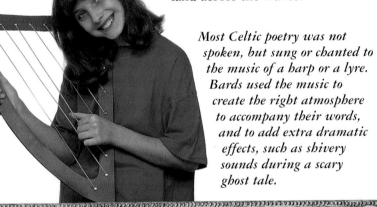

## INSPIRED BY A DREAM

While a Celtic bard sleeps, he dreams of a beautiful woman from the world of the spirits. She will be the subject of his next song. Dreams and visions were a common theme in many ancient Celtic poems and legends. For example, Oisin, son of the great hero Finn MacCool, ran away with Niamh of the Golden Hair. Niamh was a spirit who appeared to Finn in a dream and invited him to come to a magic land across the waves.

*Most Celtic poetry was not spoken, but sung or chanted to the music of a harp or a lyre. Bards used the music to create the right atmosphere to accompany their words, and to add extra dramatic effects, such as shivery sounds during a scary ghost tale.*

**4** Glue the one side of the card and and one side of the cardboard. Stick them together. Paint the harp brown and leave it in a warm place to dry.

**5** Use a bradawl to make holes approximately 5cm apart along the two straight sides of the harp. These will be the holes for the strings.

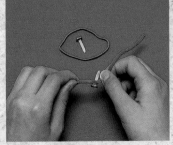

**6** Cut a length of string 40cm long. Cut 7 more pieces of string each 5cm shorter than the last. Tie a paper fastener to both ends of each string.

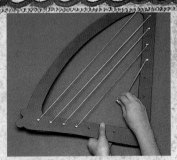

**7** Push the paper fasteners in to the harp frame so that the strings lie diagonally across the harp. Adjust the strings so that they are stretched tightly.

# Gods and Spirits

THERE ARE MANY surviving traces of Celtic religion, in descriptions by Roman writers, in carvings and statues, in place names, in collections of religious offerings, and in myths and legends. Yet there are many things we do not know or fully understand about Celtic beliefs. This is because the Celts believed that holy knowledge was too important to be written down. It seems almost certain, however, that the Celts worshipped gods who protected the tribe and gave strength in war, and goddesses who protected homes and brought fertility. Some gods were associated with the sky, and some goddesses with the earth. Gods and spirits controlled the elements and natural forces, such as water and thunder, and they were given different names in different parts of the Celtic world. Both gods and goddesses were worshipped close to water and in groves of trees. Rich offerings were left for them. The Celts believed that dreadful things would happen if they did not make sacrifices of their most valuable possessions, including living things, to the gods.

## GIFT TO THE GODS
This wooden statue is carved to look like a man wearing a Celtic hooded cloak. It was found at the source of the River Seine, in France. Small carvings like this were used to send messages to the gods.

## HANDS HELD HIGH
From the Gundestrup bowl, this bearded god holds his hands up. Such a gesture may have been used by druids (Celtic priests) when praying. The clenched fists are a sign of power.

## MAKE THE GUNDESTRUP BOWL

*You will need: plastic bowl, silver foil, scissors, cardboard strip 12cm x 84cm, felt-tip pen, modelling clay, PVA glue, double-sided tape, bradawl, paper fasteners.*

1 Find a plastic bowl that measures about 26cm in diameter across the top. Cover the bowl on the inside and outside with silver foil.

2 Use the pair of scissors to trim any excess foil, as shown. Ensure you leave enough foil to turn over the top edge neatly.

3 Divide the card into six sections. Leave 3cm at the end of the card. Draw a god figure in each section. Make a clay version of the figure. Glue it on top.

## BURIED IN A BOG

The remains of this Celtic man were found in a peat bog in northern England. He died some time between AD1 and AD200. He was sacrificed by being killed in three different ways, having been strangled, had his throat cut, and struck on the head. Like the three-mothers carving, this shows the Celts' use of the number three for religious purposes.

## HORSES AND WAR

According to Roman writers, Epona was the Celtic goddess of war. Epona was worshipped by many Roman soldiers who spent time on duty in Celtic lands. This Roman-style carving shows Epona with a horse. It was found in northern France.

## HUMAN SACRIFICE

Celtic priests, called druids, sometimes sacrificed human beings and animals as offerings to the gods. This scene from the Gundestrup bowl shows a giant-sized figure, maybe a god, holding a human sacrifice.

*The famous Gundestrup bowl, which inspired your model, was made in eastern Europe some time between 200BC and 1BC. It was found many years later in a Danish bog.*

## THREE MOTHERS

To the Celts, the number three was a sign of power, so they often portrayed their gods and goddesses in triple form. This stone carving shows three mother-goddesses. It was made in Britain, probably between AD50 and AD400. The figures stand for the three female qualities of strength, power and fertility.

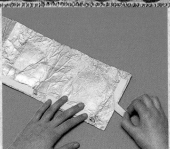

**4** Cover both sides of the card strip and the clay figures with glue. Then cover with silver foil. Make sure that the foil is well glued to the figures.

**5** Stick double-sided tape to the back of the foil-covered strip along the bottom and side edges. This will be used to join the sides of the bowl.

**6** Make holes with a bradawl every few centimetres through the bottom of the strip. Make matching holes along the top of the bowl, as shown.

**7** Attach the strip to the bowl with the double-sided tape. Stick the ends together, as shown. Secure by putting paper fasteners through both sets of holes.

# The Celtic Year

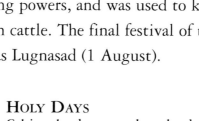

AS FARMERS, the Celts needed to be able to measure time, so that they would know when to plough their fields and sow their crops. The Celtic year (354 days) was divided into 12 months, each 29 or 30 days long. Every two-and-a-half years, an extra month was added, so that the Celts' year kept pace with the natural seasons. The Celts also marked the passing of time by holding religious festivals. Samain (1 November) was the most important. It was the beginning of the Celtic year, and was a time for sacrifices and community gatherings. It was a dangerous time, when spirits walked the earth. Samain has survived today in Christian form as All Souls' Day, and Hallowe'en. Imbolc (1 February) marked the beginning of springtime and fertility. Beltane (1 May) was observed by lighting bonfires. Their smoke had purifying powers, and was used to kill pests on cattle. The final festival of the year was Lugnasad (1 August).

### GODDESS AND SAINT
This statue is of the Celtic goddess Brigit (later known as St Brigit in Ireland) who was honoured at Imbolc. The Celts believed that she brought fertility and fresh growth. She was also the goddess of learning, and had healing powers.

### HOLY DAYS
Celtic calendars were kept by druids (priests). They believed that some days were fortunate, while others brought bad luck. This picture, painted about 150 years ago, shows how one artist thought a druid might look. However, it is mostly imaginary.

### MAKE A PIG
*You will need: modelling clay, board, modelling tool, ruler, 4 x balsa-wood sticks, metallic paint, paintbrush.*

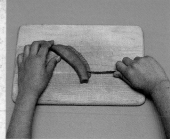

**1** Make the body of the pig by rolling a piece of modelling clay into a sausage shape roughly 13cm x 3.5cm. Make a head shape at one end.

**2** With your thumb and index finger, carefully flatten out a ridge along the back of the pig. The ridge should be about 1cm high.

**3** Now use the modelling tool to make a pattern along the ridge section. The pattern should have straight vertical lines on both sides of the ridge.

## CLEVER GOD

Archaeologists think that this stone head, found in North Wales, may represent Lug, the Celtic god of all the arts. According to legend, Lug was clever at everything. He was honoured at Lugnasad, the fourth and final festival of the Celtic year when offerings were made to all the earth spirits and goddesses, to ask them for a plentiful harvest.

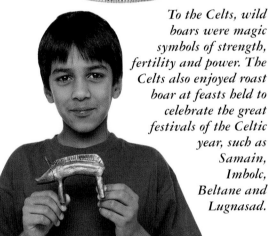

## MISTLETOE AND OAK

Both mistletoe and oak were sacred to the Celts. Druids made sacrifices at wooden temples or in sacred oak groves. Even the druids' name meant 'knowledge of the oak'. Mistletoe was magic and mysterious. It could only be cut with a golden sickle. Mistletoe growing on oak trees was the most holy and powerful of all.

*mistletoe*          *oak tree leaves*

## DRUID CEREMONY

This picture from the 1800s shows an imaginary view of druids at a Celtic religious ceremony. We have very little detailed information about how these ceremonies were performed. According to Roman writers, there were three different kinds of druids, each with different duties. Some were soothsayers, who told the future and issued warnings. Some held sacrifices. Some wrote and performed songs in honour of the gods.

*To the Celts, wild boars were magic symbols of strength, fertility and power. The Celts also enjoyed roast boar at feasts held to celebrate the great festivals of the Celtic year, such as Samain, Imbolc, Beltane and Lugnasad.*

**4** Roll out four legs roughly 4.5cm long. Push a balsa-wood stick into each leg. Leave about 1cm of balsa wood exposed, as shown.

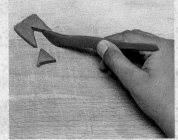

**5** Now roll out a small amount of modelling clay. Cut out two triangular shapes using your modelling tool. These will be the pig's ears.

**6** Carefully attach the ears on either side of the pig's head. Mould them on using a little water and your modelling tool, as shown.

**7** Attach the legs to the pig, pushing the balsa wood sticks into the body. Leave the modelling clay to dry. When it is dry, paint the whole pig.

# The Magic Realm

THE CELTS BELIEVED IN life after death. When a man or woman died, the soul left the body and journeyed to a magic realm of ghosts and spirits. After a time of rest in the realm, the dead person's spirit might be reborn as a new baby or, possibly, as an animal or a bird. Beliefs varied from place to place, but many Celtic peoples thought that the period soon after someone's death was a dangerous time for their relatives and friends. The dead person's spirit was trapped close to their body, and might cause harm. However, after the dead person's flesh had finally rotted away, their spirit was set free, and could help and protect people close to them. Bones from long-dead ancestors were sometimes kept by their relatives like lucky charms.

From about 700BC to 100BC, the Celts of mainland Europe buried dead bodies in the earth. Usually, the body was carefully arranged on a bed of dried grasses and flowers, dressed in clean clothes, and surrounded by treasured possessions. In the British Isles, burial customs were different. Sometimes, bodies were laid on a wooden frame in the open air until the flesh rotted away from their bones (this is called excarnation). Then the bones were buried. Sometimes, whole bodies were placed, along with others, in disused stone buildings or caves. After around 100BC, customs changed and cremation became popular throughout the Celtic world.

## FOR THE FUNERAL FEAST

When an important person died, it was the duty of their relatives to hold a funeral feast. Large quantities of wine or mead (honey wine) were served to the dead person's followers from huge kraters (mixing vessels). This krater was imported from Greece. It held 1,100 litres of wine and water.

## BURIED WITH A PRINCE

Only a very rich person could afford gold and iron in Celtic times. This golden bowl and iron dagger in a gold-plated sheath were buried in the grave of a prince at Hochdorf, in Germany, in about 540BC. The dagger's blade is bent and twisted. This may have been to 'kill' its power, so that it could rest in the grave with its owner. The prince's wife was also killed, and buried alongside her husband.

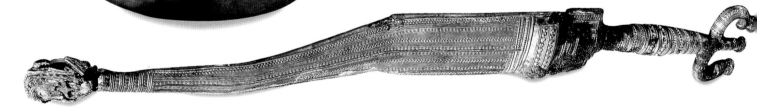

## RITUAL PIT

From around 400BC, the Celts dug deep pits at holy sites, into which they threw the remains of human bodies, sacrificed animals and offerings of pottery, wood and metal. These were probably all gifts to the gods. Most ritual pits have been found in southern France, but they have been discovered in many other Celtic lands.

## TOMB MOUND

During the Hallstatt era (750–450BC), many important Celts were buried under huge earth mounds, called barrows. Inside, there was a wood-lined burial chamber, surrounded by smaller spaces where family members could be buried later on. This picture shows an early prehistoric burial mound, based on the knowledge available to people in the 1800s and mixed with quite a lot of imagination. Today, archaeologists know that Hallstatt mounds did not have side entrances and were not surrounded by standing stones.

## LAID TO REST

This modern reconstruction shows a burial in central France, around 700BC. The dead chieftain is wrapped in a woollen blanket. Loyal followers have placed his sword and a finely-made bucket of wood and bronze nearby. A rich display of grave goods at a burial demonstrated the dead chief's wealth.

## CHANGING CUSTOMS

After cremation, the ashes of a dead person were collected up and placed in a pottery urn like this one. The pot containing the ashes was then buried in the ground. No one knows for sure why cremations replaced burials. The Celts may have come to believe that cremation made it easier for the soul to escape from the body. Or they may have been copying Roman burial customs.

# Missionaries and Monks

IN MAINLAND EUROPE, Celtic power was destroyed by AD1. From that time, the former Celtic lands were ruled by Rome. After around AD400, the Roman Empire in turn was attacked by tribespeople from beyond its frontiers. Germanic peoples, such as the Angles, Saxons and Franks, took control of north-western Europe, while the Slavs controlled east European lands. Celtic languages and artistic traditions survived for up to 200 years after the Roman invasions but, by about AD400, they had almost disappeared. In the British Isles, the situation was different. Northern and western Scotland, and the whole of Ireland, were never conquered by Rome or invaded by Germanic tribes after Roman power collapsed. Celtic languages and traditions survived there, and mingled with a new faith, Christianity (brought to the British Isles during the time the Romans ruled), to create a final flowering of Celtic culture.

## SCOTLAND'S TEACHER
Christianity first reached Ireland between AD400 and AD450, where it was spread by missionaries such as St Patrick. After St Patrick's death, Irish missionaries, including St Columba (shown here in a modern stained-glass window), carried Christian teachings to Scotland and other lands.

## ALONE TO PRAY
Leaders of the Christian Church in Ireland and Scotland encouraged men and women to live in religious communities, apart from the rest of the world, where they could devote their lives to God. Many Celtic monks built little beehive-shaped cells out of rough stone, where they could spend time alone in peace and quiet. This cell is at Cloghan, in Ireland.

## A CELTIC BORDER
*You will need: card 60cm x 40cm, ruler, pencil, felt-tip pen, paint and paintbrushes, rubber, water, water pot.*

**1** On the card draw a rectangle 57cm x 37cm. Draw lines 1cm in from the long sides and 1.5cm in from the short sides. Draw lines 9.5cm in from each end.

**2** Divide the border area you have created into two horizontally. At the far left and right ends draw lines 3.5cm in. Now draw three other lines at 7cm intervals.

**3** Begin in the top right-hand corner of the top strip. Place your pencil at the intersection of the first four rectangles. Draw the design shown above.

## IN CELTIC STYLE

The *Book of Kells* is a Christian text with Celtic decorations. It was made in about AD800, probably at the monastery on the Scottish island of Iona. The detail on some pages is so fine that it can hardly be seen by the naked eye. Books like these, written by Celtic monks in Old Irish and Latin, helped to preserve ancient Celtic words and ideas and it is thanks to these monks that so many Celtic traditions survived. As well as copying out many Christian texts, they also wrote down many ancient Celtic myths and legends, recording them for future generations to read.

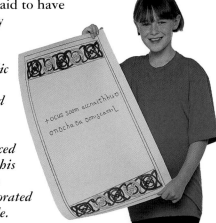

## ST MARTIN'S CROSS

Tall crosses were used to mark Christian burials, and as preaching places or border-posts on the edge of holy ground. Sometimes Celtic standing stones were turned into crosses. In other cases fresh stonework was carved. Like many other early crosses, St Martin's cross was decorated with Celtic patterns. It was made in about AD700 in Iona. There are slots cut into the ends of the crossways arms which may once have held decorative metal pieces.

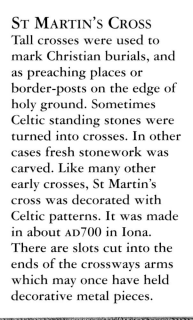

## BEAUTIFUL BOOK

The *Book of Durrow* is a Christian book decorated with Celtic designs. It was made in Iona in about AD675. Parts of it are said to have been written by St Columba.

*Copy a few Gaelic words on to your manuscript: 'And pray for Mac Craith, King of Cashell'. Interlaced designs such as this one are found in manuscripts decorated in the Celtic style.*

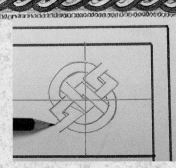

**4** Add two outer circles to your design, as shown. Join the circles to the open ends of your design to create an 'endless knot'.

**5** Add two larger circles and the corner designs to your endless knot, as shown. Extend the open ends on the left of the design to begin a second knot.

**6** Use the same method to create a row of knots. Use the grid as a guide. Next draw a row of knots in the border along the bottom of the card.

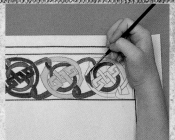

**7** Paint the different strands of knot using typical Celtic colours such as green and red. When the borders are completely dry, rub out the pencil grid.

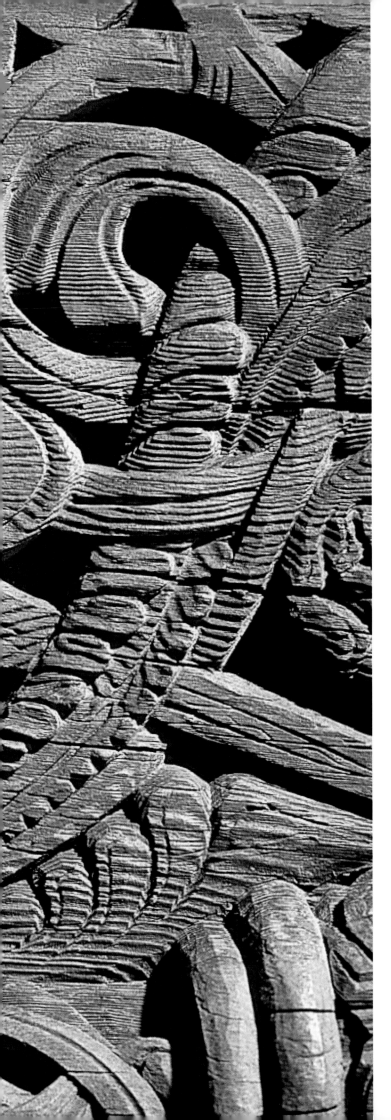

# THE VIKINGS

The Vikings were farmers, builders and metalworkers. Viking is an old Norse word meaning pirate, and the sea was the natural element of these people as they explored new lands and sailed into battle.

by
PHILIP STEELE
Consultant:
Leslie Webster, British Museum

# The Coming of the Vikings

THE YEAR IS AD795. Imagine you are an Irish monk, gathering herbs to make medicines. Walking along the river bank you hear the sound of creaking oars and curses in a strange language. Through the reeds you see a long wooden ship slipping upstream. It has a prow carved like a dragon. Inside it are fierce-looking men – battle-scarred warriors, armed with swords and axes.

Incidents like this happened time after time around the coasts of Europe in the years that followed. In the West, these invaders were called Northmen, Norsemen or Danes. In the East, they were known as Rus or Varangians. They have gone down in history as Vikings. This name comes from a word in the Old Norse language meaning sea raiding. Who were they? The Vikings were Scandinavians from the lands known today as Denmark, Norway and Sweden. Archaeologists have found their farms and houses, the goods they traded, the treasure they stole and their fine wooden ships.

### BATTLE ART
The Vikings were skilled artists, as well as fierce warriors. This Danish battle axe is made of iron inlaid with silver and decorated with swirling patterns.

### INTO THE PAST
Archaeologists have excavated Viking towns and found ships, weapons and hoards of treasure. This excavation is in York, in northern England.

### SEAFARERS
The outline of the Viking ship, with its high prow and square sail, became widely feared. This carving is from the Swedish island of Gotland.

### TIMELINE AD750–875

*The Vikings were descended from German tribes who moved northwards into Scandinavia over 2,000 years ago. They were restless, energetic people. By the 780s, they were raiding other lands. Soon they were exploring, settling and trading far from home, from North America to Baghdad. By 1100 the Vikings had become Christian and their lands had become more like the other countries in western Europe.*

*Viking sword*

AD750 Trade opens up between northern Europe and the East. Trading routes are established.

Small trading and manufacturing towns flourish, such as Ribe in Denmark, Paviken on Gotland and Helgo in Sweden.

*treasure hoard*

AD789 Vikings raid southern England.

AD793 Vikings raid Lindisfarne, an island off the north-east coast of England.

*massacre at Lindisfarne*

AD795 Vikings raid Scotland and Ireland.

AD750

AD775

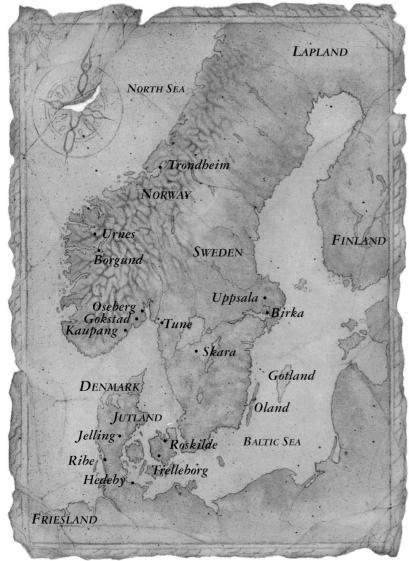

## THE VIKING HOMELANDS

The Vikings came from Scandinavia. This map shows some of the most important Viking sites. Most of these were in present-day Denmark, southern Sweden and along Norway's coastal fjords.

### INVASION FLEET

This painting shows Vikings invading England in AD866. They went on to defeat and murder Edmund, King of the East Angles. Much of our knowledge of the Vikings comes from accounts written by their enemies. Many of these, such as this one about St Edmund, were written later.

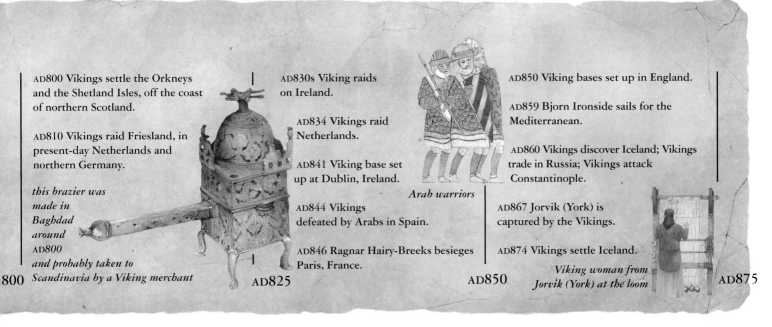

AD800 Vikings settle the Orkneys and the Shetland Isles, off the coast of northern Scotland.

AD810 Vikings raid Friesland, in present-day Netherlands and northern Germany.

*this brazier was made in Baghdad around AD800 and probably taken to Scandinavia by a Viking merchant*

AD830s Viking raids on Ireland.

AD834 Vikings raid Netherlands.

AD841 Viking base set up at Dublin, Ireland.

AD844 Vikings defeated by Arabs in Spain.

AD846 Ragnar Hairy-Breeks besieges Paris, France.

*Arab warriors*

AD850 Viking bases set up in England.

AD859 Bjorn Ironside sails for the Mediterranean.

AD860 Vikings discover Iceland; Vikings trade in Russia; Vikings attack Constantinople.

AD867 Jorvik (York) is captured by the Vikings.

AD874 Vikings settle Iceland.

*Viking woman from Jorvik (York) at the loom*

800        AD825        AD850        AD875

# The Viking World

THE VIKINGS TOOK to the sea in search of wealth, fortune and better land for farming. At that time, Denmark was mostly rough heath or woodland. The other Viking homelands of Norway and Sweden were harsh landscapes, with mountains and dense forests, which were difficult to farm.

From the AD780s onwards, bands of Vikings launched savage attacks on England, Scotland, Ireland and Wales. They later settled large areas of the British Isles, including the Orkneys, Shetlands and the Isle of Man. Viking raiders also attacked settlements along the coasts and rivers of Germany, the Netherlands and France. The area they settled in France became known as Normandy, meaning land of the Northmen.

Viking warriors sailed as far as Spain, where they clashed with the Arabs who then ruled it. They also travelled west across the Atlantic Ocean, settling in Iceland, Greenland and even North America.

Viking traders founded states in the Ukraine and Russia and sailed down the rivers of eastern Europe. They hired themselves out as the emperor's bodyguards in the city they called Miklagard – also known as Constantinople (modern Istanbul).

By the 1100s, the descendants of the Vikings lived in powerful Christian kingdoms. The wild days of piracy were over.

N

*L'Anse aux Meadows*

CANADA

NEWFOUNDLA

(VINLA

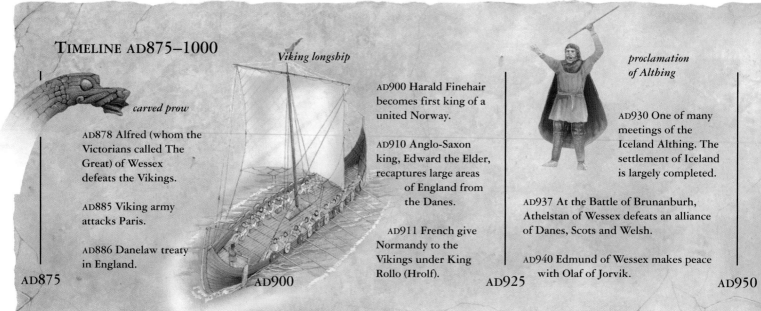

TIMELINE AD875–1000

*carved prow*

*Viking longship*

AD878 Alfred (whom the Victorians called The Great) of Wessex defeats the Vikings.

AD885 Viking army attacks Paris.

AD886 Danelaw treaty in England.

AD900 Harald Finehair becomes first king of a united Norway.

AD910 Anglo-Saxon king, Edward the Elder, recaptures large areas of England from the Danes.

AD911 French give Normandy to the Vikings under King Rollo (Hrolf).

*proclamation of Althing*

AD930 One of many meetings of the Iceland Althing. The settlement of Iceland is largely completed.

AD937 At the Battle of Brunanburh, Athelstan of Wessex defeats an alliance of Danes, Scots and Welsh.

AD940 Edmund of Wessex makes peace with Olaf of Jorvik.

AD875

AD900

AD925

AD950

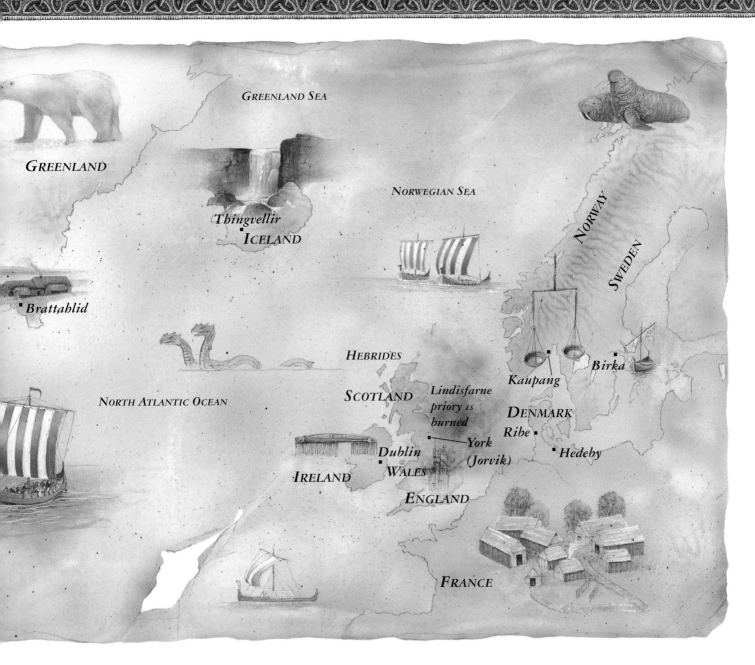

GREENLAND SEA

GREENLAND

NORWEGIAN SEA

*Thingvellir*
**ICELAND**

Brattahlid

NORWAY

SWEDEN

HEBRIDES

NORTH ATLANTIC OCEAN

SCOTLAND

*Lindisfarne
priory is
burned*

York
(Jorvik)

*Kaupang*

*Birka*

**DENMARK**
Ribe

*Hedeby*

Dublin
WALES

IRELAND

ENGLAND

FRANCE

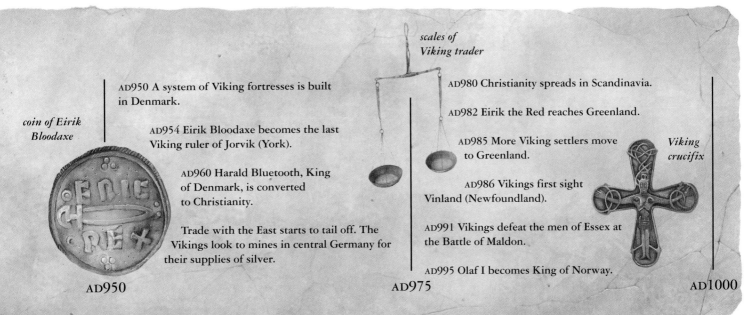

*scales of
Viking trader*

*coin of Eirik
Bloodaxe*

AD950 A system of Viking fortresses is built
in Denmark.

AD954 Eirik Bloodaxe becomes the last
Viking ruler of Jorvik (York).

AD960 Harald Bluetooth, King
of Denmark, is converted
to Christianity.

Trade with the East starts to tail off. The
Vikings look to mines in central Germany for
their supplies of silver.

AD980 Christianity spreads in Scandinavia.

AD982 Eirik the Red reaches Greenland.

AD985 More Viking settlers move
to Greenland.

AD986 Vikings first sight
Vinland (Newfoundland).

AD991 Vikings defeat the men of Essex at
the Battle of Maldon.

AD995 Olaf I becomes King of Norway.

*Viking
crucifix*

AD950

AD975

AD1000

# Viking Heroes

THE VIKINGS GREATLY admired bravery and a spirit of adventure. The names and nicknames of their heroes, who were explorers, pirates and warriors, have gone down in history. Two of the most famous were Ragnar Hairy-Breeks, who terrorized the city of Paris in AD846, and a red-bearded Norwegian called Eirik the Red, who named and settled Greenland in AD985. The Vikings we know most about were powerful kings. Harald Hardradi (meaning stern in counsel) saw his brother, King Olaf of Norway, killed in battle. He then fled to Russia and went on to join the emperor's bodyguard in Constantinople. After quarrelling with the Empress Zoë, he returned to Russia before becoming ruler of Norway.

**BLOODAXE**
This coin is from Eirik Bloodaxe's reign. He was the son of Norway's first king and ruled Jorvik (York).

Viking women could be just as tough and stubborn as their men. They were well respected, too. Archaeologists found two women buried in a splendid ship at Oseberg in Norway. One was a queen, the other her servant. They were buried with beautiful treasures.

**MEMORIAL IN STONE**
This memorial was raised at Jelling in Denmark by King Harald Bluetooth. An inscription on it says that King Harald 'won all of Denmark and Norway and made all the Danes Christians'.

**FROM WARRIOR TO SAINT**
Olaf Tryggvasön was Harald Finehair's grandson. He seized the throne of Norway in AD995. King Olaf became a Christian and was made a saint after his death in AD1000.

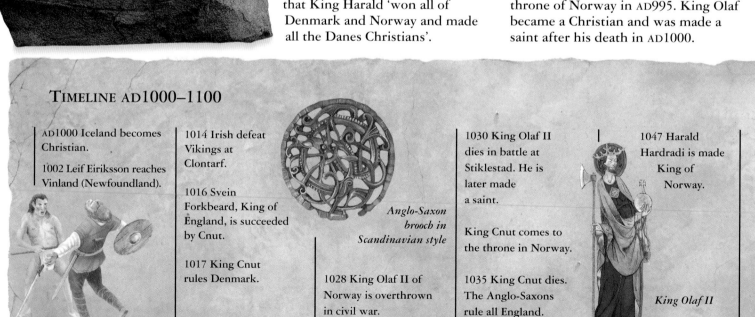

TIMELINE AD1000–1100

AD1000 Iceland becomes Christian.

1002 Leif Eiriksson reaches Vinland (Newfoundland).

1014 Irish defeat Vikings at Clontarf.

1016 Svein Forkbeard, King of England, is succeeded by Cnut.

1017 King Cnut rules Denmark.

*Anglo-Saxon brooch in Scandinavian style*

1028 King Olaf II of Norway is overthrown in civil war.

1030 King Olaf II dies in battle at Stiklestad. He is later made a saint.

King Cnut comes to the throne in Norway.

1035 King Cnut dies. The Anglo-Saxons rule all England.

1047 Harald Hardradi is made King of Norway.

*King Olaf II*

AD1000 *Viking fighting Native American in Newfoundland, North America*

AD1010

AD1020

AD1030

AD1040

AD1050

## THE NORMANS

Hrolf, or Rollo, was a Viking chief. In AD911 he and his followers were granted part of northern France by the French king. The region became known as Normandy, and the Normans went on to conquer Britain and parts of Italy.

## THE WISE RULER

Cnut was the son of Svein Forkbeard, King of Denmark. He led extremely savage raids on England, becoming king in 1016. As a king, he proved to be kinder and wiser than he had been as a warrior. By 1018 he was King of Denmark and by 1030 he had become King of Norway as well. He died at Shaftesbury in 1035.

## LEIF THE LUCKY

Leif the Lucky was Eirik the Red's son. He sailed even further west than his famous father. In about AD1000 he reached Canada, sailing to a land he named Vinland. This was probably Newfoundland. Other Vikings, including Leif's brother Thorwald, tried to settle these North American lands, but with little success.

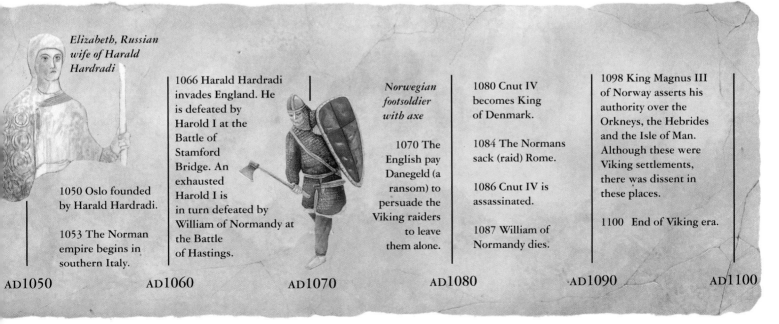

*Elizabeth, Russian wife of Harald Hardradi*

1050 Oslo founded by Harald Hardradi.

1053 The Norman empire begins in southern Italy.

1066 Harald Hardradi invades England. He is defeated by Harold I at the Battle of Stamford Bridge. An exhausted Harold I is in turn defeated by William of Normandy at the Battle of Hastings.

*Norwegian footsoldier with axe*

1070 The English pay Danegeld (a ransom) to persuade the Viking raiders to leave them alone.

1080 Cnut IV becomes King of Denmark.

1084 The Normans sack (raid) Rome.

1086 Cnut IV is assassinated.

1087 William of Normandy dies.

1098 King Magnus III of Norway asserts his authority over the Orkneys, the Hebrides and the Isle of Man. Although these were Viking settlements, there was dissent in these places.

1100 End of Viking era.

AD1050        AD1060        AD1070        AD1080        AD1090        AD1100

# Viking Society

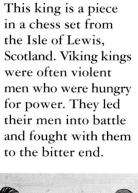

**M**OST VIKINGS WERE FREEMEN, or *karls*, who owned some land and a farm, and went to sea for raids and adventures. Other karls were merchants, ship builders or craft workers. The free Vikings used *thralls*, or slaves, as labourers and servants on farms and in workshops. Many Vikings were slave-traders. Prisoners who had been captured on raids all over Europe were sold as thralls. Viking society allowed thralls few rights. Their children were slaves as well.

The most powerful and wealthy Vikings were chieftains or *jarls* (earls). They controlled large areas of countryside. Some jarls even became local kings. Viking kings became more and more powerful as they built up new, united countries. By AD900, Harald Finehair, King of Vestfold, had managed to bring all of Norway under his control. Denmark, however, had always been ruled by a single person. In the reign of Harald Bluetooth, the country became more centralized than ever.

Yet the early Vikings had been independent, quarrelsome and proud people, and this remained true in colonies such as Iceland. Many people, including Eirik the Red, had fled there to escape the law back home. They did not like the idea of being ruled by kings from far away. Iceland remained an independent republic throughout the whole of the Viking Age. After 1100, however, it was forced to recognize a Norwegian king.

**STRONG RULERS**
This king is a piece in a chess set from the Isle of Lewis, Scotland. Viking kings were often violent men who were hungry for power. They led their men into battle and fought with them to the bitter end.

**THE FIGHTING KARLS**
Karls, or freemen, formed the backbone of a Scandinavian invasion force when the Normans attacked England in 1066. This scene is part of the Bayeux tapestry and shows Norman karls preparing for conquest.

**FARMERS**
Viking karls, or freemen, built farmhouses on the Shetland islands to the north of Scotland. The search for new land to farm led many karls to travel overseas. The buildings on Shetland were made of timber, stone and turf. Confusingly, this Viking site is known as Jarlshof today.

## LOYAL TO YOUR LORD

This reconstruction of a Viking raid is taking place on the island of Lindisfarne in northern England. Viking raiders first attacked Lindisfarne in the year AD793. A typical war band would have been made up of free men, or karls. In battle, the karls followed their jarl, or earl, into the thick of the fighting without hesitation. They formed a tight guard around him when the fighting got tough. In the early Viking days, it was more important to show loyalty to one's family or lord than to a kingdom.

## DEFENSIVE FORT

King Harald Bluetooth had a series of forts built to defend the Danish kingdom in the AD980s. This one is at Fyrkat, in Jutland. By the end of the Viking period, the days of independent Viking chieftains leading a small band of karls on a raid had all but disappeared.

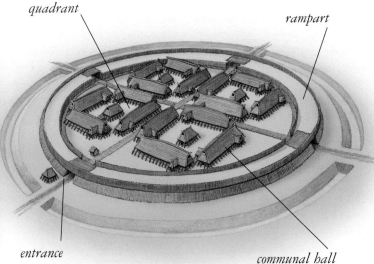

*quadrant*

*rampart*

*entrance*

*communal hall*

## A RESTLESS PEOPLE

Poor farmhands prepare wool in this reconstruction showing Vikings at work. Families of all social classes left Scandinavia to settle new lands during the Viking age. They were driven by the need for land and wealth. They faced long sea voyages and years of hard work building new farms or towns.

# Laws and Assemblies

LAWS AND JUDGEMENTS WERE passed at a public assembly called the *Thing*. This met region by region, and also in the lands where the Vikings settled. The assembly met at regular intervals and was made up only of free men. Women and slaves had no right to speak there.

The Thing had great powers, and could even decide who should be king. If someone was murdered or robbed, the victim's relatives could go to the Thing and demand justice. Everybody in the assembly considered the case. If they all agreed that a person was guilty, then judgement was passed. The person sentenced might have to pay a fine of money or other valuable goods. Sometimes the only way the dispute could be settled was by mortal combat – a fight to the death. However, mortal combat was itself made illegal in Iceland and Norway around AD1000. The assembly also dealt with arguments over property, marriage and divorce.

In Iceland there was no king at all in the Viking period. Instead, an *Althing* or national assembly was held each midsummer. The Althing was a cross between a court, a parliament and a festival. It was a chance for families to come in from their isolated farmhouses and meet up with each other. The assembly approved laws that had been drafted by the jarls and elected a Law Speaker.

**PAY UP**
The Thing could order a criminal to pay the victim, in the form of money or goods. If the criminal failed to do so, he was made an outlaw. This entitled anyone to kill him.

**THE PLACE OF LAWS**
The Icelandic Althing met on the Thingvellir, a rocky plain to the east of Reykjavik. A Law Speaker read out the laws, which had been passed by a group of 39 chieftains, from the Law Rock. The Althing is the world's oldest surviving law-making assembly on record. It met from AD930 until 1800 and again from 1843. Today it is Iceland's parliament.

### A Difficult Decision

This carving shows an important gathering of the Althing in AD1000. The assembly was split over a difficult decision – should Iceland become Christian? It was left to the Law Speaker to decide. After a lot of thought, he ruled that the country should be officially Christian, but that people who wished to worship the old gods could do so in private.

### Manx Law

This earth mound marks the site of the old Viking assembly on the Isle of Man. The Vikings who settled on this island, off the west coast of Great Britain, called this assembly field the Tynwald. This is also the name of the island's parliament today. The Tynwald still has the power to make the island's laws.

### Mortal Combat

A Viking duel is re-enacted today. Life was cheap in Viking times and violent death was common. A fight to the death was an official way of settling a serious dispute, such as an accusation of murder. This system of justice was taken to England by the Normans in 1066.

### Law Makers

Viking chieftains would ride to Iceland's Thingvellir (Assembly Plain) from all over the island. This 19th century painting by W G Collingwood shows chieftains assembling for the Althing. This assembly was held only once a year.

# The Gods of Valholl

THE EARLY VIKINGS believed that the universe was held up by a great ash tree called Yggdrasil. The universe was made up of several separate worlds. Niflheim was the underworld, a misty realm of snow and ice. The upper world was Asgard, home of the gods. Its great hall was called Valholl (Valhalla), and it was here that warriors who died bravely in battle came to feast. The world of humans was called Midgard. It was surrounded by a sea of monsters and linked to Asgard by a rainbow bridge. Beyond the sea lay Utgard, the forest home of the Giants, deadly enemies of the gods.

The Vikings believed in many gods. They thought that Odin, father of the gods, rode through the night sky. Odin's wife was Frigg (a day of the week – Friday – is named after her) and his son was Baldr, god of the summer Sun. Powerful, red-bearded Thor was the god of thunder. Like many of the Vikings themselves, he enjoyed laughing, but was quick to anger. The twins Frey and Freya were god and goddess of fertility and love. Trouble was stirred up by Loki, a mischief-making god.

### WORSHIPPING FREYA
This silver charm shows Freya. She was the goddess of love and marriage and was particularly popular in Sweden. Freya was the sister of Frey, the god of farming. It was also believed that when women died, Freya would welcome them into the next world. In *Egil's Saga*, a dying woman says 'I have not eaten and shall not till I am with Freya'.

### THOR'S HAMMER
This lucky charm from Iceland shows Thor. He used his magic hammer to fight the giants. Thor was strong and brave.

### BALDR IS SLAIN
Stories tell how the wicked Loki told the blind god Hod to aim a mistletoe spear at Baldr, god of the Sun and light.

---

### MAKE A LUCKY CHARM

*You will need: thick paper or card, pencil, scissors, self-drying clay, board, felt-tip pen, modelling tool, rolling pin, fine sandpaper, silver acrylic paint, brush, water pot, a length of cord.*

**1** Draw the outline of Thor's hammer onto thick paper or card and cut it out. Use this as the pattern for making your lucky charm, or amulet.

**2** Place a lump of the clay on the board and roll it flat. Press your card pattern into the clay so that it leaves an outline of the hammer.

**3** Remove the card. Use a modelling tool to cut into the clay. Follow around the edge of the imprint as shown, and peel away the hammer shape.

## SLEIPNIR

Odin rode across the sky on Sleipnir, a grey, eight-legged horse. A pair of wolves travelled with Odin. In this carved stone from Sweden, Odin and Sleipnir are arriving at Valholl. They would have been welcomed by a *valkyrie*, or servant of the gods, bearing wine for Odin to drink.

## ODIN

One-eyed Odin was the wisest of all gods. He had two ravens called Hugin, meaning thought, and Mugin, meaning memory. Each day the ravens flew across the world. Every evening they flew back to Odin to perch on his shoulders and report to him the deeds that they had seen.

*Vikings wore lucky charms or amulets to protect themselves from evil. Many of the charms, such as this hammer, honoured the god Thor.*

**4** Model a flattened end to the hammer, as shown. Use a modelling tool to make a hole at the end, to thread the cord through when it is dry.

**5** Use the end of a felt-tip pen, a pencil or modelling tool to press a series of patterns into the clay, as shown. Leave the clay to dry and harden.

**6** When the amulet is dry, smooth any rough edges with sandpaper. Paint one side silver. Leave it to dry before painting the other side.

**7** When the paint has dried, take enough cord to fit your neck and thread it through the hole in the hammer. Cut it with the scissors and tie a knot.

# The Coming of Christianity

BY THE BEGINNING of the Viking Age, most of western Europe had become Christian. The early Vikings despised the Christian monks for being meek and mild. The warriors looted church treasures on their raids and murdered many priests or sold them into slavery. However, over the years, some Vikings found it convenient to become Christian. This made it easier for them to trade with merchants in western Europe and to hire themselves out as soldiers with Christian armies.

Christian missionaries went to Scandinavia from Germany and the British Isles. Monks from Constantinople preached to the Vikings living in the Ukraine and Russia. They soon gained followers. In about AD960, King Harald Bluetooth of Denmark became a Christian. In AD995, Olaf Tryggvason, a Christian king, came to the throne of Norway. He pulled down many of the shrines to the old gods. In AD1000, the Viking colonists on Iceland also voted to become Christian. The new faith spread from there to Greenland. Sweden was the last Viking country to become Christian. People gave up worshipping pagan gods in the old temples of the settlement at Uppsala.

**NEW FAITH**
This silver crucifix was found in the Gotland region of Sweden. It is nearly 1,000 years old. It shows Christ wearing breeches, like those worn by Viking men.

**STAVE CHURCH**
This Christian church is made of staves, or split tree trunks. It was built in Gol, in Norway, in about 1200. The very first Christian churches in Scandinavia were built in this way. When the wooden foundations rotted away, the churches were rebuilt.

**SIGN OF THE CROSS**
This stone was raised at Jelling in Denmark by King Harald Bluetooth, in honour of his parents. It dates from about AD985. The stone marks a turning-point in Viking history – the conversion of the Danes to Christianity. One side of the stone shows a dragon-like beast fighting with a snake. The other side is a Christian scene (*above*), showing Jesus on the cross.

_crucifix_

_Thor's hammer charms_

## CHOICE OF GODS

The mould below was made from a soft mineral called soapstone. It was used to shape metal pendants 1,000 years ago. The mould could produce both hammer-of-Thor designs and crosses (*above*). The two religions – the old and the new – existed side-by-side for many years in the Viking world. It was a long time before Christianity really took hold. Many of the early converts to Christianity still turned to Thor for help in the heat of battle.

_mould_

## AGAINST EVIL

Is this a silver cross, or a hammer-of-Thor charm with a dragon's head? Perhaps it was both. It was certainly intended to protect the wearer from evil and bad luck. Even after they became Christians, the Vikings remained very superstitious people. Helgi the Lean is described in a Viking saga as believing in Christ 'yet he still asked Thor for help on sea voyages and when facing danger'.

## BAPTISM IN A BARREL

The Danish king, Harald Bluetooth, was converted to Christianity in about AD960. This gold altar piece shows Harald being baptised in a barrel of holy water by Bishop Poppo. Harald went on to build a Christian church on the ancient site of the royal burial mound at Jelling.

## STONE CROSS

This cross is from Kirkinner Church, in Scotland. It is about 1,000 years old. Its carving shows a mixture of Anglian and Norwegian Viking styles. The Christians in Britain, France and Germany were horrified by the Vikings' pagan religion, and they tried to persuade them to give it up. Eventually, Viking kings saw that becoming Christian could make them more powerful.

# Settlements and Towns

**HEDEBY**
This is a model of Hedeby, an important market town, now in modern Germany. This area used to be part of Denmark. At its peak in AD950, Hedeby was home to more than 1,000 people.

THE WORLD in which the Vikings lived was not as crowded as ours. Many families lived in farmhouses far from their neighbours. Some lived in small settlements on the shores of remote deep sea inlets called *fjords*. The Vikings built small towns when they settled new lands or set up trading posts. These towns were usually ranged around a waterfront by the sea or a river, where ships could moor for loading. The smell of fish would hang in the air, accompanied by the sound of squabbling gulls. Away from the waterfront, the town would usually be defended by a ring of earthworks and wooden stockades. It might be attacked at any time.

Viking merchants' town houses were often built of timber planks or of wattle and daub (a criss-cross design of sticks covered with clay or dung). Houses had fenced yards or gardens, where chickens, geese and pigs were kept. Fresh water came from wells and springs. The streets were lined with market stalls selling goods. They were unpaved, but lengths of timber were laid down to stop them getting too muddy. Rubbish was thrown onto a midden or tip. There was no proper drainage. Towns must have been unhealthy and smelly places. Sewage went straight into holes dug in the ground or it was dumped in a large pit called a cesspit.

**WALLS OF STONE**
Building materials depended on local supply. These stone ruins mark the outlines of an ancient Viking settlement on the Brough of Birsay. This tiny island lies on the shores of mainland Orkney, whose Viking name means 'island of seals'. The Orkney islands, off the north coast of Scotland, were settled by the Vikings from the year AD800.

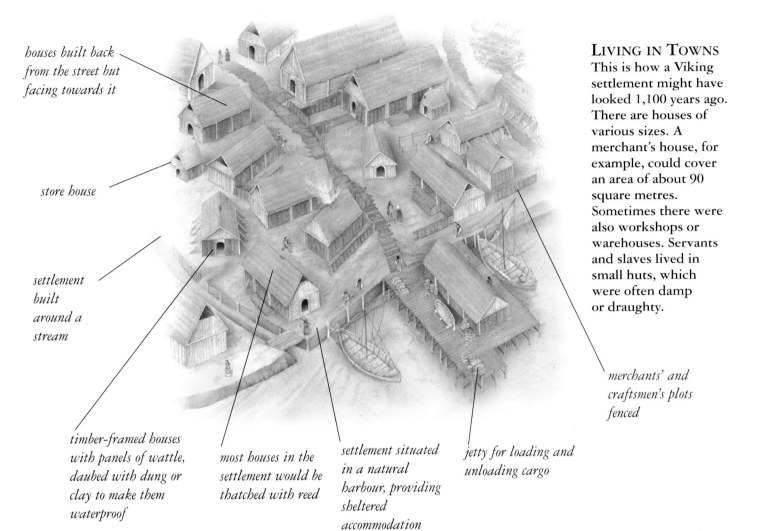

houses built back
from the street but
facing towards it

store house

settlement
built
around a
stream

timber-framed houses
with panels of wattle,
daubed with dung or
clay to make them
waterproof

most houses in the
settlement would be
thatched with reed

settlement situated
in a natural
harbour, providing
sheltered
accommodation

jetty for loading and
unloading cargo

merchants' and
craftsmen's plots
fenced

## LIVING IN TOWNS

This is how a Viking settlement might have looked 1,100 years ago. There are houses of various sizes. A merchant's house, for example, could cover an area of about 90 square metres. Sometimes there were also workshops or warehouses. Servants and slaves lived in small huts, which were often damp or draughty.

## UNCOVERING A TOWN

Archaeologists excavate a Viking town house at the settlement of Jorvik (York), in England. The oldest houses in Jorvik were made of wattle, twigs tightly woven around upright posts. Oak planks were used in later Viking buildings. The stones in the foreground are part of an old hearth.

## TURF CONSTRUCTION

In countryside settlements, timbers or stones were often covered with a thick layer of turf. This acted as the roof and walls. These Viking farmhouses have been rebuilt at Glaumber, in Iceland.

# The Longhouse

THE MOST TYPICAL Viking houses were farmsteads, built in the countryside. At the centre of the farming settlement was a large building called the longhouse. This was a low building up to 30 metres in length, which was usually built of timber. Stone boulders were used on islands, such as Iceland, where there was a shortage of trees. Roofs were thatched or covered with a layer of turf.

Early in the Viking Age, longhouses were basic. Family and farmworkers lived together in a single great hall. There was even a section for the animals under the same roof. People huddled around the central fire to keep warm. Later, longhouses often had extra rooms, such as a bedroom for the farmer and his wife, a room for spinning and weaving wool, and a dairy where the women made butter and cheese. There was sometimes a separate kitchen, a food store and a bath house. Toilets were simple earth pits dug off the main hall. Outbuildings included byres and barns where the animals were kept in winter. Farm tools and weapons were repaired in a workshop.

**GREEN ROOF**
This reconstructed Icelandic home has wattle-and-daub walls. The roof is covered with thick strips of turf, to keep out the cold. The grass on the roof turf keeps growing.

**DANISH DWELLING**
This longhouse was reconstructed at Trelleborg in Denmark. It is similar to the style of the fortress longhouses that stood here in AD900. These buildings had long, curved roofs covered in wooden tiles. Historians now believe that the pillars on this reconstruction are not accurate.

## MAKE A HOUSE

*You will need: thick card, ruler, pencil, scissors, balsa wood, craft knife, paintbrushes, brown, white and black acrylic paints, masking tape, PVA glue, brush, pet shop straw, sandpaper.*

10cm
7cm
front door

*To decorate:* 12 x strips of balsa wood 6-7cm long.

walls x2
6cm
14cm

15cm
roof
5.5cm

10cm
base
20cm

back
7cm
10cm

Ask an adult to cut out thick card pieces for the base, walls and roof of the house using the measurements above (templates not shown to scale).

**1** Paint all the walls of the house brown and leave them to dry. Using a piece of card as a guide, pick out the wattle-and-daub pattern with white paint.

**2** Paint in wooden planking above the door and leave to dry. Stick balsa wood strips around the door and gables and on the side walls, as shown.

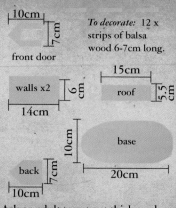

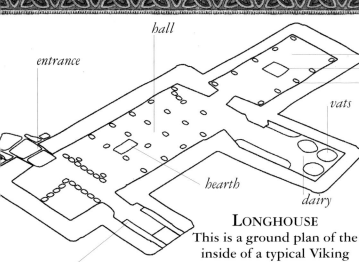

entrance

hall

living room

hearth

benches

vats

hearth

dairy

lavatory

### LONGHOUSE

This is a ground plan of the inside of a typical Viking farmhouse. It is based on the Stöng house in Iceland.

### THE CUTTING EDGE

This Viking axehead was found at Jorvik (York) in England. Axes were used for clearing the land for a new settlement. They were also used to fell timber for building and for fuel.

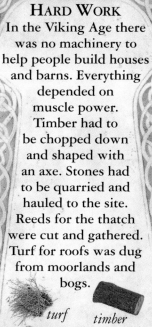

### HARD WORK

In the Viking Age there was no machinery to help people build houses and barns. Everything depended on muscle power. Timber had to be chopped down and shaped with an axe. Stones had to be quarried and hauled to the site. Reeds for the thatch were cut and gathered. Turf for roofs was dug from moorlands and bogs.

turf        timber

stone       straw

### HOME FROM HOME

This is where Eirik the Red and his wife Thjodhild built their Greenland home over 1,000 years ago. They built their longhouse from stone. Life in the Greenland settlements was very harsh.

*The Vikings adapted to their surroundings by using whatever materials were available locally for their houses. In Denmark wood was used. However, in Greenland stone was more plentiful.*

**3** Paint the base brown and allow to dry thoroughly. Glue the walls in position on the base. Use masking tape to secure them while the glue dries.

**4** Tape layers of straw thatch onto the roof section. (Instead of using real straw you could chop off the bristles from a decorating brush.)

**5** Finish off the roof. Continue building up layers of thatch with straw. Make sure that the layers are even to give the roof a good finish.

**6** Stick on the thatch roof. Tear sandpaper into pieces and glue onto the base to look like rough turf. Glue balsa strips on to the base as a pathway.

# Inside a Viking Home

T HE LIGHT WAS DIM inside a Viking house. There might be just one small window with wooden shutters and no glass. The air indoors would have been sharp with smoke from burning logs or a peat fire. The fire burned in a central hearth made from stone. There were no chimneys, so the smoke from the fire drifted out through a hole in the roof.

In the houses of wealthy families, the wooden walls and beams were sometimes beautifully carved. Tapestries might hang on the walls, but there were no carpets. Instead, sweet-smelling rushes were scattered on the earth floor. They were swept away when they became soiled. Built-in ledges around the walls were used for sitting on by day and sleeping on by night. In later times, rich people might have owned a special bed, which would have been finely carved. Mattresses were filled with down or with straw. The bed covers were woollen blankets or warm furs.

There was much less furniture than in a typical modern home. Weapons, tools and clothes were hung from the wall or stored in large chests. Jewellery or money could be hidden away in strongboxes or caskets. Foodstuffs, such as butter, salted fish or flour and drinks, such as ale, were stored in buckets, barrels and tubs.

**FLICKERING LIGHT**
Small lamps were placed on tables or hung from the ceiling. They were carved from soapstone and filled with oil and a wick. Working indoors was hard. A lamp like this would have given out poor light that flickered in the draught.

**CENTRAL HEARTH**
This picture of a 100 year old hearth shows how cauldrons of hot food would have simmered over the fire in an Icelandic farmhouse. The hearth was at the centre of every Viking home, providing light and warmth.

## MAKE A DRINKING HORN

*You will need: thick paper, pencil, ruler, scissors, mug, masking tape, brown paper, self-drying clay, newspaper, water, PVA glue and brush, paints, paintbrush, silver foil.*

**1** Cut the paper into strips 28cm in length, but different widths. Roll the widest strip into a ring using the rim of a mug as a guide. Bind the edges with tape.

**2** Next roll up the next widest strip, and bind it with tape. Place it inside the first. Make more rings, each one slightly smaller than the previous one.

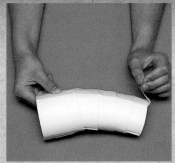

**3** Place each of the smaller rings into the slightly larger one before it, binding with tape. You are making the tapered shape of a curved horn.

### ROYAL BED

A princess or queen slept in this fine bed. It was found in a ship buried in Norway. Only the rich would have had beds and separate bedrooms. Ordinary people slept on benches spread with rugs.

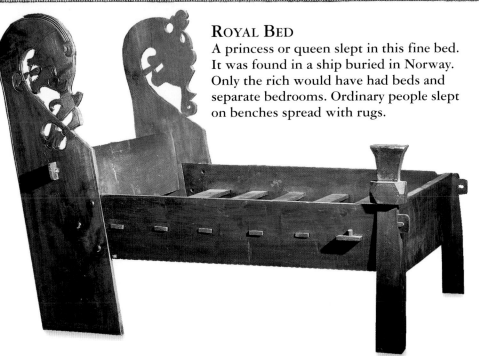

### LOCK UP YOUR LOOT!

Keys, such as these, were used to lock a chest. This is where a Viking would have kept precious things, such as daggers or silver.

### AT HOME IN YORK

This is a reconstruction of a Viking home in Jorvik. Baskets and bags hang from the ceiling and a large barrel sits in the corner. An old man warms himself by the hearth. No doubt he is telling tales of exciting sea voyages in his youth, or complaining about his aches and pains!

*Viking drinking horns were filled for a toast with mead, a drink made from honey, water and yeast.*

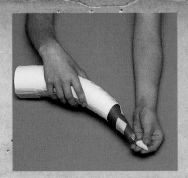

**4** Roll the brown paper into a cone to make the horn's pointed end, and bind it in position. Round off the sharp end with clay. Leave it to dry and harden.

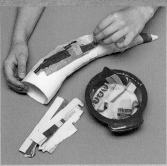

**5** Cover the horn in papier mâché. Cut strips of newspaper, soak them in water and glue them to the horn. Leave to dry and then add more layers.

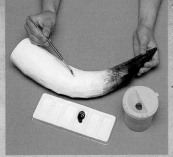

**6** When the papier mâché is dry, paint the horn. To look real, the main part of the horn should be white, with the tip painted brown and black.

**7** Cut the silver foil into a pattern and glue it to the rim of the horn. Real Viking drinking horns were often beautifully decorated with silver.

# Family Life

EVEN IN MODERN ICELAND, everybody seems to know who is related to whom and where they live. In Viking times too, a large number of relatives played their part in the family, including grandparents, aunts and uncles. They were all very aware of family links, and loyalty was fierce. If one member of a family was harmed, then the other members of the family would seek revenge. This led to feuds – quarrels between one family and another that simmered on from one generation to the next. Feuds led to fights, theft and sometimes even as far as murder.

The father of the household had great power over other members of the family. If he thought a newborn baby was a weakling, he could leave it to die. When a Viking farmer died, his eldest son inherited the farm. The rest of the family would have to move away, and the younger sons would have to find new land of their own to farm. Mothers were often strong, determined women who had great influence in the family. There was little schooling. Learning how to fight with a sword or use an axe was more important than reading and writing. As children grew up, they were expected to work hard and to help around the house. They were sometimes fostered out to families on other farms and had to work in return for their keep.

### HELPING OUT
This reconstruction of a market stall in Jorvik shows a young lad helping his parents during a day's trading. Children often followed in the same trade as their parents. This boy would have learnt how to haggle over prices. He would also know how to weigh silver.

### FAMILY MEMORIALS
The Vikings often put up memorial stones to honour relatives and friends when they died. This stone from Sweden was put up by Tjagan and Gunnar in loving memory of their brother Vader.

## LIVING IN FEAR

Old tales tell how Vikings fought each other mercilessly during long, bitter feuds between families. Murderous bands might turn up at a longhouse by night, threatening to burn down the roof and kill everybody inside. Viking households also risked attack from local peoples or other raiders wherever they settled.

## WANTING CHILDREN

A woman who wanted to make a good marriage and have children would pray to Frey, the god of love and fertility. On these gold foil charms from Sweden, Frey is shown with his beautiful wife Gerda. She was the daughter of a giant called Gymir.

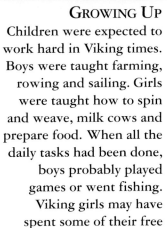

## GROWING UP

Children were expected to work hard in Viking times. Boys were taught farming, rowing and sailing. Girls were taught how to spin and weave, milk cows and prepare food. When all the daily tasks had been done, boys probably played games or went fishing. Viking girls may have spent some of their free time gathering berries and mushrooms.

## BURIAL GRAVE

This skeleton belongs to a Viking woman from Iceland. Archaeologists have been able to tell how women lived in the Viking age by examining the goods placed in their graves. These were possessions for them to use in the next world.

# Viking Women

**V**IKING WOMEN could not speak at the assembly, yet they had more independence than many European women of their day. They could choose their own husband, own property and be granted a divorce. At a wedding, both the bride and groom had to make their marriage vows before witnesses. Memorial stones show that many husbands loved their wives and treated them with respect.

Women certainly needed to be tough in the harsh landscapes and cold climates of countries such as Iceland or Greenland. It was their job to make woollen or linen clothes for the family, to prepare and cook food and to clean the home.

It was the women who usually had to manage the farm and its workers while their men were off raiding or trading. They never knew if their husbands, brothers and sons would return from the wars in the British Isles or be lost in a storm at sea.

**WELCOME HOME**
A woman in typical Viking dress welcomes a warrior returning from the wars. She has long hair tied back by a scarf and is wearing a pleated dress. The woman is a valkyrie, one of Odin's maidens in Valholl. This charm comes from Öland in Sweden.

**A DAY'S WORK**
In this reconstruction from Jorvik (York), a Viking woman goes out to fetch water from the well. Hissing geese beat their wings and scatter in her path. Women's work lasted from dawn till nightfall, with clothes to darn, poultry to look after, meals to cook and children to scold! Most women also spent several hours a day spinning and weaving wool into cloth to make clothes.

## PRACTICAL BUT PRETTY

Viking women wore long tunics fastened by a pair of brooches. This Viking brooch was found in Denmark. It is over 1,000 years old and is made of gold. Women wore clothing that was both practical and comfortable.

## GETTING READY

Before a wedding or a visit to the fair, a Viking woman may have smoothed or pleated her dress on a board like this one. A glass ball would have been used instead of an iron. This whalebone board comes from Norway.

## WEAVING AT HOME

Viking looms were like this one. The warps, or upright threads, hang from a crossbar. The weft, or cross threads, pass between them to make cloth. Weaving was done by women in every Viking home.

## THE NEW QUEEN

This picture shows Queen Aelfgyfu alongside her husband King Cnut, in England. Aelfgyfu was Cnut's second wife. They are placing a cross on an altar. Queens were the most powerful women in Scandinavian society.

## BELOVED WIFE

This stone was put up by King Gorm as a monument to his wife. The inscription reads 'King Gorm made this memorial to his wife Thyri, adornment of Denmark'. The messages written on such stones show the qualities that Vikings admired most in women.

# Dress and Decoration

Typical dress for Viking women and girls was a long shift. It was made of wool or linen. Over this they wore a woollen tunic, with shoulder straps secured by ornate brooches. Between the brooches there was often a chain or a string of beads. Sometimes a chain dangled by their side, holding keys. Men and boys wore long breeches and knee-length woollen tunics with sleeves. Brightly coloured clothes were popular with both sexes.

Trade with Asia brought richer cloths, such as fine silk, to the Viking homelands. Woollen cloaks and caps were worn to keep out the winter cold. Shoes and boots were flat and made of leather. Viking men often wore beards. Both men and women had their hair long. Hair could be tied back with a band. Women often plaited or knotted their long hair, or tucked it under a head scarf.

## HAIR CARE
Both Viking men and women took great care of their long, flowing hair. The combs they used were often made of horn from the antlers of red deer. Many combs were beautifully carved.

## BOOTS AND SHOES
Viking cobblers made slippers, shoes and boots of calfskin or goatskin. Footwear was often laced with a leather thong. New soles were sewn on when the old ones were completely worn through. These shoes were discovered in the city of Jorvik (York).

The Vikings loved showy jewellery, especially rings, armbands and gold and silver necklaces. These were often decorated with ornate designs. Jewellery was a sign of wealth and could be used instead of money to buy things.

## MAKE A BROOCH

*You will need: self-drying clay, rolling board, string, PVA glue and brush, bronze paint, water, paint brush, compasses, tracing paper, pencil, ruler, gold foil, scissors, card, safety pin.*

1 Take a ball of clay and mould it into a brooch shape, as shown. The brooch should be about 2–3cm in diameter. Leave it in a warm place to dry.

2 Place glue round the edge of the brooch and carefully stick string around outside as shown. This will make a border for the Viking brooch.

3 When the brooch is dry, paint it carefully with bronze acrylic paint. Paint the string border, too. Leave the brooch in a warm place to dry.

## PRECIOUS AMBER

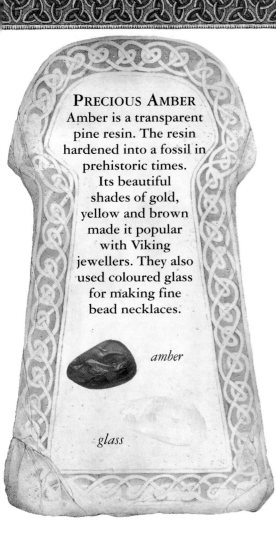

Amber is a transparent pine resin. The resin hardened into a fossil in prehistoric times. Its beautiful shades of gold, yellow and brown made it popular with Viking jewellers. They also used coloured glass for making fine bead necklaces.

*amber*

*glass*

## GOLD AND JEWELS

This hoard of gold and jewellery was hidden away in Norway in the 800s. It includes fine rings and necklaces and other precious items from France, England and Arab countries. Most of it would have been looted or raided. Such items were sometimes worn, or melted down for sale.

## BURIED SILVER

This beautiful Viking brooch was found in a hoard buried in northern England. It is over 1,000 years old and is made of silver. Brooches were used to fasten cloaks and dresses.

## SOCKS

This Viking sock was found at Jorvik (York). Cloth and fabric is not found very often because these materials usually rot more quickly than metal or stone. The few items that have been found were preserved in waterlogged soil.

*Brooches were important pieces of jewellery – and not only for decoration! They were used as fasteners for cloaks and tunics.*

4 Use compasses to draw two brooch-sized circles on paper. Draw a common Viking pattern in your circles or trace one from a book.

5 Trace the patterns on to a piece of gold foil. Take care not to tear the foil. Cut the patterns out in small pieces that will interlink.

6 Glue the pieces of foil pattern on to the outside of one of the brooches and leave to dry. Repeat with the other brooch.

7 Cut and stick a circle of card on to the back of each brooch. Fix a safety pin to the back of each brooch with masking tape. Your brooch is now ready!

# Farming and Fishing

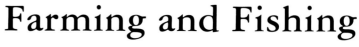

THE VIKINGS ARE so famous as warriors and pirates that we sometimes forget that they mostly lived by farming and fishing. Their best farmland lay in Denmark and southern Sweden. Viking settlers overseas had to make do with some very poor soils and harsh climates. Pigs and poultry were kept in most farmyards. Viking farmers also raised sheep, goats and cattle. In Norway, herds of cows were led to mountain pastures during the summer and brought down to the farmstead for the winter. Many cattle were slaughtered as winter set in and their meat was preserved by salting, drying or smoking. Crops grown by Viking farmers included grains such as wheat, barley and oats. Flax was grown in warmer regions, such as Denmark, and was made into linen. Farm tools were home-made from wood and iron, and included hoes, picks, shovels, scythes, sickles and shears. Thralls, or slaves, toiled away clearing forests, digging, threshing and harvesting.

### VIKING PONIES
These tough little ponies are from Iceland. The ponies that were bred by the Vikings in Iceland, the Shetland Isles and northern Scandinavia grew a warm winter coat. They grazed on turf and were fed hay in the winter. They were used for carrying peat and other heavy loads, and for riding.

### HARVEST OF THE SEA
Fishermen used both nets and barbed metal fish hooks, such as these, to snare their catch. All kinds of freshwater fish could be had from lakes and rivers. The Baltic Sea, North Sea and North Atlantic Ocean provided them with fish such as herring and cod. Fishbones found in Viking middens, or rubbish tips, show that fish formed a major part of the diet.

### FISHING BOAT
Fishing scenes such as this would have been common in the fjords of Norway and along the coast of Iceland. This carving is from Cumbria in northern England. It shows the god Thor and the giant Hymir fishing for the serpent of Midgard.

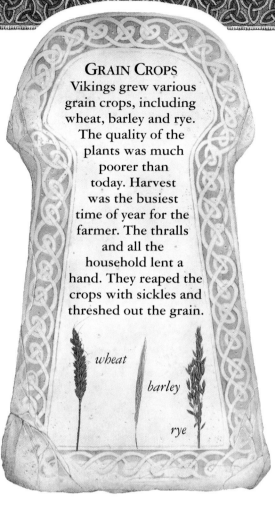

## GRAIN CROPS

Vikings grew various grain crops, including wheat, barley and rye. The quality of the plants was much poorer than today. Harvest was the busiest time of year for the farmer. The thralls and all the household lent a hand. They reaped the crops with sickles and threshed out the grain.

*wheat*

*barley*

*rye*

## HAVE YOU ANY WOOL?

This modern reconstruction from Jorvik (York) shows a Viking shepherd boy and his sheepdog, with a newly shorn fleece. Wool was the main fabric for cloth-making.

## WORKING THE LAND

This springtime scene, embroidered on a wall hanging from Bayeux, Normandy, shows a man ploughing with horses and another sowing. Spring was the busiest time of year for the Viking farmer.

# Food and Feasts

A Viking family ate twice a day. The food was usually prepared at the central hearth, although some large farmhouses had separate kitchens. Chiefs held long, drunken feasts in their great halls, and wedding celebrations could go on for weeks.

Oats, barley and rye were made into bread and porridge. The hand-ground flour was often coarse and gritty and poor people added peas and bark to make it go further. The dough was mixed in large wooden troughs and then baked in ovens or on stone griddles. Goat, beef and horse meat were all popular and would be roasted over the fire or stewed in cauldrons. Hunting provided venison, reindeer, wild boar, wildfowl and hare. Honey was used to sweeten dishes, as sugar was still unknown in Europe. It was also used to make a strong alcoholic drink called mead. Wines were made from fruits and berries. Beer made from barley was gulped down from the hollowed-out horns of cattle.

## VES HEILL!
'Be healthy!' was the toast in old Iceland. Vikings swigged their ale from drinking horns. These were often beautifully decorated with ornate metal bands.

## BRING ME WINE!
A group of Norman lords drink wine from horns, in England in 1086. The Normans had invaded England 20 years before. They were descendants of Hrolf and the Vikings who had been given lands in France in 911. Norman life was still centred around the great hall in which banquets were held.

## ON THE TABLE
Bowls and platters were made of wood. Spoons were made of horn or metal. People picked up meat in their fingers and cut it with a sharp knife or dagger – there were no forks.

## MAKE A VIKING LOAF
*You will need: sieve, mixing bowl, 225g white flour, 115g wholemeal flour, 1 teaspoon baking powder, 1 teaspoon salt, 150g edible seeds, 475ml warm water, wooden spoon or spatula, baking tray.*

**1** First wash your hands. Then begin by sifting together the white flour and the wholemeal flour through a sieve into a mixing bowl.

**2** Sprinkle 1 teaspoon of baking powder and 1 teaspoon of salt into the sifted flour. Adding salt will help to give flavour to your Viking loaf.

**3** Stir half of the seeds into the bowl. Sunflower seeds give a crunchy texture to the loaf, but you could use any other edible seeds.

## VIKING TASTES
The quality of Viking vegetables was probably not as good as that of those available today. Cabbages and peas used by Viking cooks were tough and stringy. Seeds, garlic and herbs, such as dill and coriander, were used to add flavour to many dishes. Many of these herbs grew wild.

*dill*

*coriander*

## DRINK IT UP!
These cups and jug would have been on the table of a merchant in the Swedish town of Birka. They may have held water, wine or mead. A lot of pottery was imported into Scandinavia from Germany and the lands to the south.

*The Vikings used seeds and split peas to add flavour and bulk to bread. Sunflower seeds make a tasty modern substitute.*

4 Add 2 cups of warm water and stir well with a wooden spoon or spatula. At this stage the mixture should become quite stiff and hard to stir!

5 Use your hands to knead the mixture into a stiff dough. Sprinkle some flour on to your hands, to stop the mixture sticking to them.

6 When the dough is well kneaded and no longer sticky, place it on a greased baking tray. Sprinkle the rest of your seeds on top of the loaf.

7 Put the baking tray in a cold oven. Turn the oven to 190°C (Gas 5) and cook the bread for 1 hour. Cooking the bread from cold will help it to rise.

# Land Transport

IN THE VIKING AGE, roads were mostly in poor repair, or were little more than muddy tracks. The Vikings made roadways by sinking timbers into the ground. They often built causeways across marshy ground. In many areas it was quicker to travel around the coast by boat than to cross mountains or moors in poor weather. In northern lands, snow and ice made winter travel difficult, although the Vikings were highly skilled at overcoming icy conditions.

The Vikings were good at riding. They used horses for travel and transport as well as in battle. Horses carried baggage and pulled wheeled carts and covered wagons. Sledges were also used to carry goods. They could be hauled over grass or soil as well as ice and snow. Carts and sledges found in the Oseberg ship burial were beautifully carved. The ones used every day were probably much plainer. The Vikings used skis, skates and snowshoes for travelling cross-country in winter.

### CARVED SLEDGE
No less than four wooden sledges were found in the grave of the Viking queen buried at Oseberg in Norway. They were designed to be pulled by a horse. Three of the sledges were richly decorated.

### RIDING OFF TO WAR
This silver figure shows a Viking warrior on horseback, carrying a sword. It was found at the market town of Birka in Sweden and is over 1,000 years old. The Vikings were skilled horsemen.

### RIDING TACKLE
During the Viking Age, stirrups arrived in Europe from Asia. They began to be widely used by horse riders. Other remains of riding tackle discovered by archaeologists have included spurs (*above*), saddles, bridles and harnesses. They were often beautifully made.

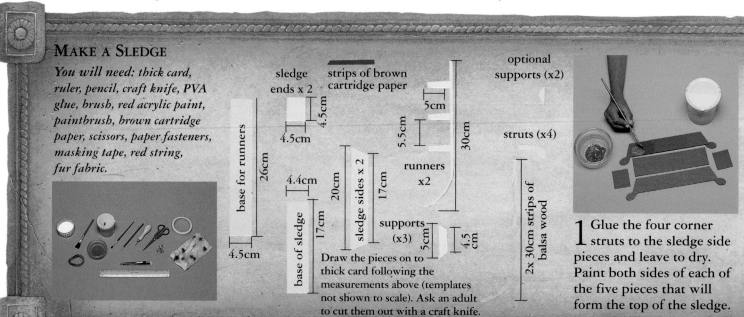

### MAKE A SLEDGE
*You will need: thick card, ruler, pencil, craft knife, PVA glue, brush, red acrylic paint, paintbrush, brown cartridge paper, scissors, paper fasteners, masking tape, red string, fur fabric.*

sledge ends x 2

strips of brown cartridge paper

optional supports (x2)

5cm

5.5cm

struts (x4)

30cm

base for runners

26cm

4.5cm

4.5cm

4.4cm

20cm

sledge sides x 2

17cm

runners x2

17cm

base of sledge

supports (x3)

5cm

4.5 cm

2x 30cm strips of balsa wood

4.5cm

Draw the pieces on to thick card following the measurements above (templates not shown to scale). Ask an adult to cut them out with a craft knife.

1 Glue the four corner struts to the sledge side pieces and leave to dry. Paint both sides of each of the five pieces that will form the top of the sledge.

## HORSE POWER

Surviving bridles and harnesses show how horses became more and more important to the Vikings. The descendants of the Vikings in northern France – the Normans – were among the first warriors on horseback in Europe.

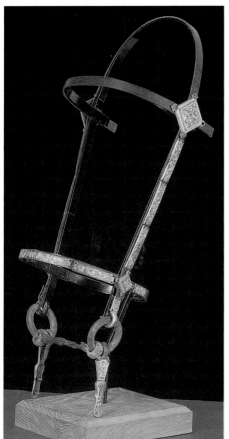

## WOODEN WAGONS

This royal wagon was found in the Oseberg ship burial. It is covered in rich carvings. Similar ones can be seen on a tapestry found at Oseberg. The upper bodies of wagons like these could be taken off the carriage. They were sometimes used as coffins.

## SITTING PRETTY

This is a saddle bow. It was found at Jorvik (York). It is decorated with silver and strips of horn. A bow is the raised ledge at the front and back of a saddle, which gives support to the rider.

*Imagine a young Viking princess, wrapped in warm furs, riding over the snow and ice on a sledge like this.*

**2** Cut several strips of brown cartridge paper. Arrange the strips to form diamond patterns along the sides of the sledge. Trim them and glue in place.

**3** Ask an adult to make holes with a bradawl. Push paper fasteners through to form patterns. Glue the top of the sledge. Hold it together with masking tape.

**4** While you wait for the top to dry, glue the 8 pieces that form the base of the sledge together. Glue the 2 supports on to strengthen the base.

**5** Paint the base red and leave it to dry. When it is completely dry, brush plenty of glue down each side and carefully slide the top onto it. Leave it to dry.

# All Kinds of Ship

T HE VIKINGS DEPENDED on the sea. It served as a highway for them. Ships were used for transport around the islands and fjords wherever they settled. Fish, seals and whales from the sea provided food, oil, skins and bone. The Vikings were masters at seafaring and were among the most skilful ship builders the world has ever seen.

The most famous Viking vessel was the longship. It could be up to 23 metres in length. This long, sleek sailing ship was used for ocean voyages and warfare. It was still shallow enough to row up a river. The longship had an open deck without cabins or benches. The rowers sat on hide-covered sea chests that contained their possessions, weapons and food rations. The Vikings built many other kinds of ship. They had broad-beamed ships for carrying cargoes up and down the coast, as well as small rowing and sailing boats for transport and fishing. The ships were all built to fine, curved designs, with high prows and sterns.

## SAILING AWAY
This picture from a stone on Gotland, in Sweden, shows a small, two-man boat. Like larger Viking ships, it has a rectangular sail, a single mast and a broad steering oar towards the stern. The outlines of ropes and rigging can be made out, too.

## CRESTING THE WAVES
The *knarr* was a trading vessel, designed for the open ocean. It had a covered deck at each end. The central hold could be filled to the brim with bales of wool. On board it might have had a small four-oared boat called a *færing*. This little boat could be used for a day's fishing in the fjord.

*knarr*

*færing*

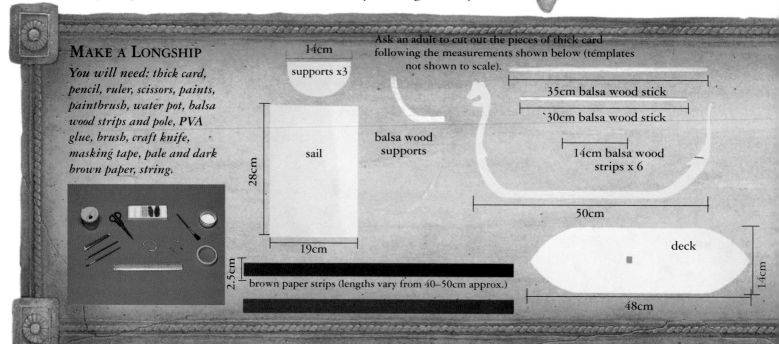

## MAKE A LONGSHIP
*You will need: thick card, pencil, ruler, scissors, paints, paintbrush, water pot, balsa wood strips and pole, PVA glue, brush, craft knife, masking tape, pale and dark brown paper, string.*

Ask an adult to cut out the pieces of thick card following the measurements shown below (templates not shown to scale).

14cm

supports x3

sail

28cm

19cm

2.5cm

brown paper strips (lengths vary from 40–50cm approx.)

balsa wood supports

35cm balsa wood stick

`30cm balsa wood stick

14cm balsa wood strips x 6

50cm

deck

14cm

48cm

## GOKSTAD SHIP

Royal ships have been excavated from Norwegian burial mounds at Gokstad and Oseberg. These funeral ships were beautifully made, but were not really designed for long ocean voyages.

## BUILDING A FLEET

This is part of the Bayeux tapestry, from Normandy. It shows boats being built for the invasion of England in 1066. The Normans built ships the way their Viking ancestors would have done. Carpenters cut the oak planks with an axe and drilled them with a tool called an auger.

## A ROYAL SHIP

This picture shows what the ship that was excavated from Gokstad would have looked like. Being a royal ship, it was built of the finest oak. It had a pine mast.

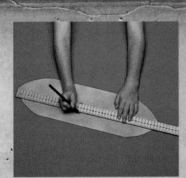

**1** Paint the deck shape light brown on one side and black on the other. When it is dry, mark out the planks lengthwise 5mm apart.

**2** Glue balsa wood cross support 'planks' on to the brown side of the deck as shown. Ask an adult to cut a hole in the deck with a craft knife, for the mast.

**3** Turn the deck over. Measure and cut three more balsa wood planks. Glue them in position, matched with the planks on the other side.

**4** Cut and glue three semi-circular pieces of card for the crossbeams.

*continues overleaf*

# The Longship

Viking longships were built in the open air, on a beach or river shore. A single oak beam was used for the keel – the backbone of the ship. The keel was 18 metres or more in length. Iron nails and washers were used to fix the long, wedge-shaped planks to the frame. Longships were 'clinker-built', which means that each of the layers of planking, or strakes, overlapped the next. Another strong beam of wood supported the mast. This, together with the cross-beams, strengthened the frame of the boat. The planks were caulked (made watertight) with a stuffing of wool or animal hair. They were coated with a tar made of pine resin. Oar holes in the top strake ran the length of a longship. A broad steering oar was secured by thongs to the starboard (right-hand side) of the stern. The pine mast could be lowered. It supported a large square or rectangular sail made of heavy woollen or linen cloth. The sail was often patterned in stripes. The ship's simple rigging was made of hemp or sealskin ropes.

## DRAGON SHIPS

The high prow of the Viking longship was often beautifully carved. This replica ship has a fierce dragon as its figurehead. Carvings like these were probably meant to scare off evil spirits. They certainly scared the enemy!

**5** Carefully draw and cut out the pieces for the keel of the boat. Paint one side red and leave to dry. Then paint the other side of the keel.

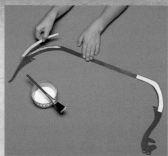

**6** When the paint is completely dry, glue the pieces of balsa wood to the curved parts of the keel to strengthen them. Leave them to dry.

**7** When the glue is dry, measure then make three slots along the length of the keel with a pair of scissors for the deck crossbeams to slot into.

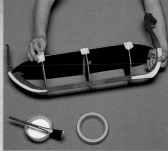

**8** Slip the deck crossbeams into the slots on the keel pieces. Glue them in place. Bind them with masking tape to hold them while they dry.

## MODERN VIKINGS

Modern ship builders have built replicas of longships, either for tourist voyages or to find out how well they sailed. These new longships have proved to be strong, fast and easy to sail. The planking bends well to the waves and is light enough for the ship to be hauled overland.

## SHIPS' TIMBERS

In the Viking Age, much of northern Europe was still densely forested. In most places there was no shortage of timber for building or repairing longships. Oak was always the shipbuilders' first choice of wood, followed by pine, beech and ash.

*beech*

*oak*

## PUTTING TO SEA

A longship put to sea with a crew of 30 or more fighting men. Each one would have to fight the enemy as well as man the oars. The warriors' round shields were sometimes slung or slotted along the side of the ship. An awning of sailcloth could be erected to keep off the sun or rain.

*Journeys by longship could take their Viking crew far and wide.*

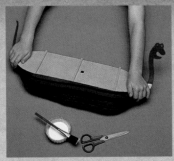

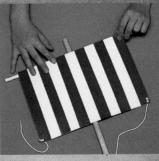

**9** Cut strips of pale and dark brown paper for the planks; or 'strakes', along each side of the keel. Carefully glue a strip in position along each side.

**10** Continue gluing strips in place. Alternate pale and dark brown strips. Trim the strips as they get lower so that they form a curve.

**11** Ask an adult to help you to cut two pieces of balsa wood pole. Glue them together. When the glue is dry, bind them with string.

**12** Cut out a square sail and paint it with red and white stripes. Glue it to the mast and attach some string rigging. Paint a dragon on the prow.

# Seafaring and Navigatio

**L**ONGSHIPS WERE SPEEDY vessels. They were capable of sailing from Scandinavia to North America in under a month. Most voyages, however, were long and harsh and interrupted by storms and battles. There were supplies of fresh water on board. The food for the voyage included anything that could be easily stored, such as apples, cheese and dried meat. Fish could be caught along the way to provide fresh food for the sailors. Warriors usually slept on board the ship. Sometimes they ran the ship on to the beach and camped on shore.

The Vikings understood winds, currents and tides better than any other seafarers in Europe at that time. When possible, they followed coastlines with known landmarks. When they crossed open ocean, they had to steer their ships by the Sun and stars. They often sketched out simple maps of coastlines and landmarks to use as charts for their long voyages.

Longships were often blown off course by storms. This was how the Vikings first discovered North America. A seafarer called Gunnbjorn was blown within sight of Greenland in about AD920. This was 60 years before it was colonized by Eirik the Red. The Canadian coast was discovered by accident in about AD985 by a lost seafarer called Bjarni Herjolfsson. This was 17 years before the expedition of Leif Eiriksson, known as Leif the Lucky.

**A FAIR WIND**
Gilded bronze weather vanes, like this one, topped the mast of many Viking ships. Sailors watched them for a change in the wind direction. This vane was later set up on the roof of a Swedish church.

**VIKING GRAFFITI**
This sketch of a dragon-headed longship was scratched on to wood long ago by an unknown Viking. Today it is in the National Maritime Museum at Bergen, in Norway.

## MAKE A WIND VANE

*You will need: stiff card, pencil, pair of compasses, ruler, bradawl, gold acrylic paint, paintbrush, water pot, brass hinges, balsa wood, wood screws, screwdriver, gold card, PVA glue, brush.*

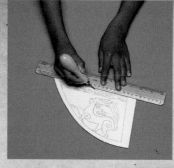

**1** Draw a line across a piece of card. Draw a shorter vertical line at a right angle. Use compasses to draw a line to make the curved shape of the vane.

**2** Cut out the wind vane. Then use a bradawl to score lines in the card. Make up your own Viking pattern or copy the one shown here.

**3** Cover the work surface to protect it. Paint the patterned card with a light, even layer of gold paint on one side. Leave it to dry. Paint the other side.

## OUT OF THE STORM

This painting shows a Viking invasion fleet running before a strong wind across the North Sea. The awnings are raised against the driving rain and salt spray. Fleets of longships could be large. It was said that 300 of them could anchor in the harbour of the Jomsberg Viking fortress in Denmark.

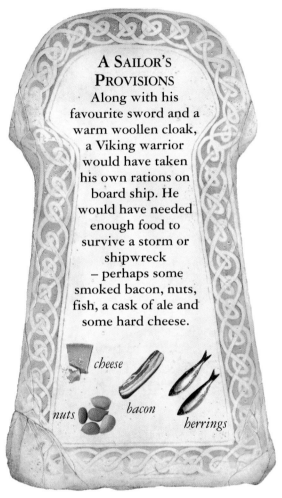

### A SAILOR'S PROVISIONS

Along with his favourite sword and a warm woollen cloak, a Viking warrior would have taken his own rations on board ship. He would have needed enough food to survive a storm or shipwreck – perhaps some smoked bacon, nuts, fish, a cask of ale and some hard cheese.

*cheese*

*nuts*  *bacon*

*herrings*

## THE VINLAND MAP

This map includes Europe, North Africa, Greenland and Vinland, the area known now as Newfoundland. The Vinland map is said to have been copied in about 1440 from an original Viking map. However, most experts believe this map is a fake, produced in modern times.

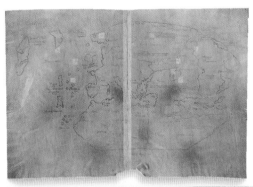

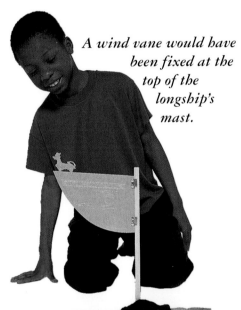

*A wind vane would have been fixed at the top of the longship's mast.*

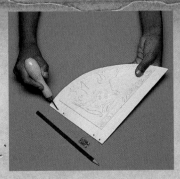

**4** Place the hinges under the short border of the card. Push the point of the bradawl through the hinges, boring four holes through the card.

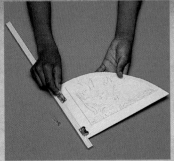

**5** Cut a balsa wood mast. Ask an adult to help you to screw the wind vane to the mast using the brass hinges and some wood screws.

**6** Draw the shape of a real or imaginary bird or animal, such as a raven or dragon, on to the back of some gold card. Cut it out carefully.

**7** Glue the gold bird or animal to the upper edge of the vane. Leave it to dry. Your Viking wind vane is ready and now all you need is a good breeze!

# Traders and Merchants

THE VIKINGS were second to none as successful merchants. Their home trade was based in towns such as Hedeby in Denmark, Birka in Sweden and Kaupang in Norway. As they settled new lands, their trading routes began to spread far and wide. They traded in countries as far apart as Britain, Iceland and Greenland.

In about AD860, Swedish Vikings opened up new routes eastwards through the lands of the Slavs. They rowed and sailed down rivers such as the Volga, Volkhov and Dniepr. Viking sailors hauled their boats around rapids and fought off attacks from local peoples. Their trade turned the cities of Holmgard (Novgorod) and Könugard (Kiev) into powerful states. This marked the birth of Russia as a nation. Merchants crossed the Black Sea and the Caspian Sea. They travelled on to Constantinople (Istanbul), capital of the Byzantine empire, and to the great Arab city of Baghdad.

Viking warehouses were crammed with casks of wine from Germany and bales of woollen cloth from England. There were furs and walrus ivory from the Arctic and timber and iron from Scandinavia. Vikings also traded in wheat from the British Isles and rye from Russia.

**COINS**
These silver coins were found on the site of the market place in Birka. They were minted in Hedeby in around AD800.

**MAKING MONEY**
This disc is a die – a metal stamp used to punch the design onto the face of a coin. The die is from York, in England. It has a sword design.

**AMBER KING**
This carved amber king is a piece from a board game. Amber was exported from the lands around the Baltic Sea. It was much prized by traders and by craftworkers, who also made it into jewellery and lucky charms.

## MAKE A COIN AND DIE

*You will need: self-drying clay and tool, board, rolling pin, scissors, pair of compasses, pencil, paper, PVA glue, brush, paintbrush, bronze and silver paint.*

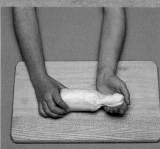

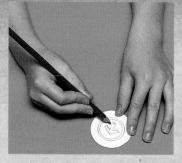

1 Roll out a large cylinder of clay and model a short, thick handle at one end. This is the die. Leave it in a warm place to harden and dry.

2 Cut out a circle from paper. It should be about the same size as the end of the die. Draw a simple shape on the paper circle, with a pencil.

3 Cut the paper circle in half. Cut out the shape as shown. If you find it hard to cut the shape out, you could ask an adult to cut it out with a craft knife.

## EASTERN CONNECTIONS

Trade networks in the East linked up with older routes, such as the 'silk road' to China. Silk, jewellery and spices were brought by camel from the Far East. In Baghdad's markets, Vikings bought these things in return for furs, beeswax and slaves.

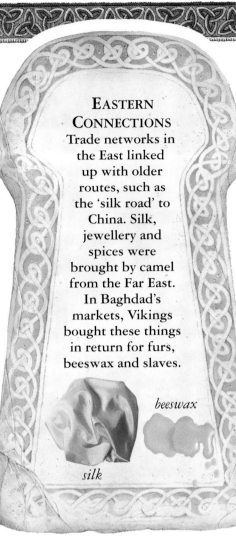

*beeswax*

*silk*

## TRADE MAP

The routes taken by Viking traders fanned out south and east from their homelands. As well as exotic goods from the East, everyday items such as salt, pottery and wool were brought back from western Europe.

*scales*

*weights*

*The first coins to show Viking kings were minted in England.*

## FAIR TRADING

Scales and weights were used by merchants wherever they traded. Some could be folded up inside a small case.

*scales*

**4** Glue the cut paper pieces on to the end of the die with PVA glue. You may need to trim the pieces if they are too big to fit on the end.

**5** Viking dies would have been made of bronze, or some other metal. Paint your die a bronze colour. Make sure you paint an even coat.

**6** Roll out some more clay. Use the die to stamp an impression into the clay. This is your first coin. You can make as many as you like.

**7** Use a modelling tool to cut around the edge of the coin. Make more coins from the left-over clay. Let the coins harden and dry and then paint them silver.

# Raids and Piracy

In AD793, a band of heavily armed Vikings ran their longships ashore on Lindisfarne (an island off the coast of Northumbria, in England). This was the site of a Christian monastery. The monks tried in vain to hide their precious crosses, their silver chalices and Bibles. The Vikings axed them down, set fire to the buildings and sailed away with their loot.

This was the start of the period in which the Vikings spread terror around western Europe. They began by attacking easy targets, such as villages, monasteries, or other ships. They took away cattle or grain, chests of money and church bells that could be melted down. They also took women and slaves. The booty was shared out among members of the crew.

Soon the Vikings were attacking the largest and richest cities in Europe. In AD846 they sacked, or raided, the cities of Hamburg and Paris. King Charles the Bald of France had to pay the Viking leader Ragnar Hairy-Breeks over three tonnes of silver to leave. From AD865 onwards the English kings were also forced to pay huge sums of money, called Danegeld. Like gangsters, the Vikings returned time after time, demanding more money – and land on which they could settle.

**BLOOD AND FIRE**
This gravestone is from Lindisfarne. It shows fierce Viking warriors armed with swords and battle axes.

**INVADING VIKINGS**
This painting shows Danish Vikings invading Northumbria. The raiders soon realized how easy it was to attack neighbouring lands. They began to set up year-round war camps on the coasts. Soon they were occupying large areas of territory and building their own towns.

## SAFE AND SOUND

Gold, silver and jewellery were locked up in beautiful caskets and chests. This copy of a Viking chest is made of walrus ivory and gilded bronze.

## ST CUTHBERT

This picture from the Middle Ages shows St Cuthbert praying in the sea. Cuthbert was one of Lindisfarne's most famous monks. He was made a saint on his death in AD687. In AD875, when the Danish Vikings attacked the island, the monks fled inland to safety, carrying St Cuthbert's remains.

## BUILT FROM THE RUINS

In AD793, the Vikings sacked the monastery on Lindisfarne, an island off the coast of northeast England. Afterwards, the religious buildings lay in ruins. The new priory pictured here was built between AD1100 and 1200. The stones used to build it were taken from the ruins left by the Vikings. Today, only bare stones remain to remind visitors of the original monastery and its terrible fate.

## TREASURE HOARD

This is part of a hoard of about 40kg of Viking silver. It was found in a chest in Cuerdale, England. The Cuerdale hoard included chopped-up silver ready for melting down, fine brooches and coins from all over the Viking world. Hoards of loot, or wealth, were often buried or hidden away for safety.

# The Viking Warrior

**SILVER FACE**
Bearded and bold – is this the face of a warrior? This lucky charm, made in silver, was worn on a chain around the neck.

Tʜᴇ ᴇᴀʀʟʏ Vɪᴋɪɴɢ ᴡᴀʀʀɪᴏʀs were mostly farmers. They turned their hand to fighting whenever a raiding expedition was organized. Some Vikings became mercenaries – full-time fighters who hired out their services. Later in the Viking Age, kings could conscript, or call up, soldiers to fight a war.

Viking warriors fought hard. To die in battle was their greatest glory – it made sure of their welcome by the gods in Valholl. Leading warriors worked themselves up into a frenzy before battle. They were called *berserkir*, named after their bearskin cloaks.

Much of the fighting took place in skirmishes, ambushes and surprise attacks. In battle, warriors let loose waves of arrows and spears and then charged the enemy lines. Hand-to-hand fighting was brutal. Swords clashed, axes were swung, heavy shields thudded together. There was kicking, biting, bloody wounds and cracked skulls. Viking warriors fought to the bitter end.

**SEA WOLVES**
The Vikings' enemies wrote of them as if they were packs of wolves, pouring out of the north. They were often cruel and violent, but nobody doubted their extraordinary courage.

**BERSERK!**
This grim-faced warrior, known as a *berserkir*, is a pawn in a chess set. He is shown in the rage of battle, biting into his shield. This walrus ivory piece was found on Lewis, an island off the coast of Scotland.

## MAKE A VIKING HELMET

*You will need: tape measure, balloon, petroleum jelly, newspaper, PVA glue, scissors, ruler, card, pair of compasses, water pot, thick brush, fine brush, bronze acrylic paint.*

1 First make the main part of the helmet. Use a tape to measure around your head. Blow up a balloon to the same size as your head. Tie the end.

2 Cover half of the balloon in petroleum jelly. Next apply papier-mâché. This is made by soaking newspaper strips in water and glue.

3 Allow the papier-mâché to dry out and harden. Now burst the balloon. Trim off the ragged edges with scisssors until the helmet is neat and round.

### THE HORSEMAN

This early stone carving shows a mounted warrior with his sword, shield and hound. While Vikings usually fought battles on foot, they were as skilled at fighting on horseback as they were on board ships. Horses were to play an increasingly important part in later Viking and Norman victories.

### SHIELD BY SHIELD

Viking warriors could use their shields to form a defensive wall or as a heavy wedge to break up the enemy lines.

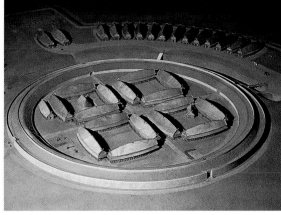

### THE FORTRESS

This model shows the earth ramparts of Trelleborg, on the Danish island of Sjælland. It was one of four great forts probably built by Harald Bluetooth in about AD980. It would have included barracks and provided shelter for local people in times of warfare.

*The wealthier Viking chieftains could afford metal helmets that protected the face from swords and battle axes. A Viking in battle must have been a scary sight.*

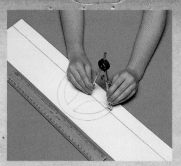

**4** Measure and cut a piece of card long enough to fit around the base of the helmet. Use compasses to draw semicircular patterns on the card, as shown.

**5** Cut out the faceguard pattern and glue it onto the rim of the helmet. Cut and glue two long strips of card over the top of the helmet, as shown.

**6** When the glue has dried, you can cover the whole helmet in bronze paint. Use a thick brush for the first coat. Then leave the helmet to dry.

**7** Use a fine brush to fill in any unpainted areas in the papier-mâché to give a neat finish. Make sure the paint is dry before you try the helmet on!

# Weapons and Armour

V IKING WARRIORS WERE not like soldiers in an official army. They were not supplied with armour and weapons. They wore their own clothes and brought their own equipment to the battle. Most warriors wore caps of tough leather. Where metal helmets were worn, these were usually conical and they sometimes had a bar to protect the nose. Viking warriors wore their everyday tunics and breeches and cloaks to keep out the cold. A rich jarl might possess a *brynja*, which was a shirt of mail, made up of interlinking rings of iron. The heavy round shield, about one metre across, was made of wooden planks. It had an iron boss (central knob) and a rim of iron or leather.

On board the longship were spears of various weights, longbows, deadly arrows and long-shafted battle axes. The most prized personal weapon of all was the Viking sword, which often had a beautifully decorated hilt. The blades of the swords were either made by Scandinavian smiths or imported from Germany. To make a sword, a smith would heat up bars of iron, twisting them and beating them into a long blade. Separate cutting edges of tough steel were welded to the blade afterwards.

### SPEARHEAD
This Swedish spearhead is made of bronze and its socket is decorated with silver. Broad-bladed spears were designed to be held in the hand. They were used for stabbing. Lighter narrow-bladed spears were used for throwing.

### NEW STYLES
This Norwegian knight appears on a tapestry made in about 1180. At the end of the Viking Age, the Normans introduced a long, kite-shaped shield. This was used by the first knights of the Middle Ages, who also wore the mail shirt and a metal helmet with a nasal (nosepiece).

### MAKE A SHIELD
*You will need: card, scissors, ruler, string, pencil, pair of compasses, gold and red acrylic paints, paintbrush, paper bowl, newspaper, masking tape, PVA glue and brush, foil, paper fasteners, craft knife, stick, bias binding.*

**1** Draw a small circle in the centre of the card with compasses. Then use a length of string tied to a pencil to draw the big circle, as shown above.

**2** Cut out the large circle from the card. Then add a design such as the one shown here. Finally paint the shield and leave it to dry.

**3** Use a paper party bowl for the shield's central boss, or knob. Scrunch up some newspaper into a flattened ball and tape it to the top of the bowl.

## SWORDS AND AXES

These weapons from Jorvik (York) include the remains of two Viking swords with double-edged blades. The iron spearhead would have been fitted onto a light wooden shaft. The Vikings used various axes for hacking the enemy at close range or for throwing from a distance.

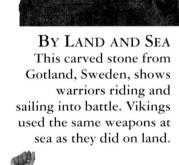

## WEAPON PARTS

Metal stirrups and weapons have been excavated by archaeologists in many parts of the Viking world. The wood has often rotted away. The iron spearheads and axeheads have survived but not the wooden shafts to which they were fitted.

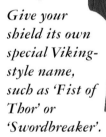

## BY LAND AND SEA

This carved stone from Gotland, Sweden, shows warriors riding and sailing into battle. Vikings used the same weapons at sea as they did on land.

## BRONZE HELMET

Goods found in Swedish graves show how wealthy chieftains lived before and during the Viking age. This pre-Viking helmet has a bronze cap with a pattern of warriors, and cheek guards of iron. Most Viking helmets were much less ornate.

*Give your shield its own special Viking-style name, such as 'Fist of Thor' or 'Swordbreaker'.*

**4** Spread glue over the bowl and then cover it with foil. An iron boss would have strengthened the shield and protected the warrior's hand.

**5** Glue the boss to the centre of the shield. Secure the boss with paper fasteners punched through the edge and through the card of the shield.

**6** Ask an adult to cut a hole with a craft knife in the back of the shield. Glue the stick to the back. Add strips of tape to make it extra secure.

**7** Attach the bias binding to the rim of the shield using small dabs of glue (or you could use paper fasteners). Your shield is now ready for battle.

# Craftworkers

### SNARL OF THE DRAGON
This masterpiece of wood carving and metalwork is a dragon-head post. It is from the Oseberg ship burial in Norway and dates from about AD850. Its patterns include monsters known as 'gripping beasts'.

IN EVERY VIKING HOME people turned their hand to craft work. The men made and repaired tools and weapons. They carved walrus ivory and wood during long winter evenings. The women made woollen cloth. They washed and combed the wool and then placed it on a long stick called a distaff. The wool was pulled out and spun into yarn on a whirling stick called a spindle. The yarn was woven on a loom, a large upright frame. Blacksmiths' furnaces roared and hammers clanged against anvils as the metal was shaped and re-shaped.

Professional craftworkers worked gold, silver, bronze and pewter – a mixture of tin and lead. They made fine jewellery from amber and from a glassy black stone called jet. Beautiful objects were carved from antlers and ivory from the tusks of walruses. Homes, and later churches, had beautiful wood carvings. Patterns included swirling loops and knots, and birds and animals interlaced with writhing snakes and strange monsters.

### SWIRLS OF SILVER
This elegant silver brooch was found in Jutland, Denmark. If you look closely, you can see a snake and a beast in the design. The brooch belongs to the late Viking Age.

### MAKE A SILVER BRACELET

*You will need: tape measure, self-drying clay, board, scissors, white cord or string, modelling tool, silver acrylic paint, paintbrush, water pot.*

**1** Measure your wrist with the tape measure to see how big your bracelet should be. Allow room for it to pass over your hand, but not fall off.

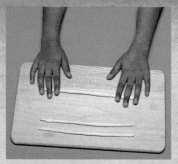

**2** Roll the clay between the palms of your hand. Make three snakes that are just longer than your wrist measurement. Try to make them of equal thickness.

**3** Lay out the three snakes on the board in a fan shape. Cut two lengths of white cord, a bit longer than the snakes, and place them in between.

## COLOURS FOR CLOTH

Woollen cloth was dyed in bold colours from leaves, roots, bark and flowers. A wildflower called weld, or dyer's rocket, was used for its yellow dye. The root of the madder gave a red dye. Bright blue came from the leaves of woad plants.

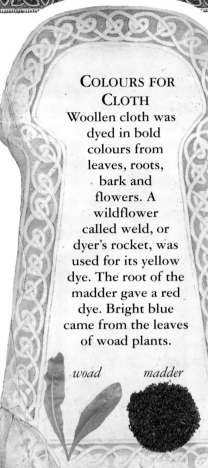

*woad*    *madder*

## THE SMITH AT WORK

This fine wood carving comes from a church in Urnes, Norway. It shows Regin the blacksmith forging a sword on an anvil, for the legendary hero Sigurd. The smith is using bellows to heat up the furnace. The skills of metal working were so important in ancient times that smiths were often seen as magical figures or gods.

## TOOLS FROM THE FORGE

Viking blacksmiths used hammers for beating and shaping metal. Tongs were used for handling red-hot iron. Shears were for cutting metal sheets. The blacksmith made everything from nails and knives to farm tools.

*Vikings liked to show off their wealth and rank by wearing expensive gold and silver jewellery.*

**4** While the clay is still soft, plait the snakes of clay and the two cords together. Ask an adult to help if you are not sure how to make a plait.

**5** Trim each end of the plait with a modelling tool. At each end, press the strands firmly together and secure with a small clay snake, as shown above.

**6** Carefully curl the bracelet round so that it will fit neatly over your wrist, without joining the ends. Leave it in a safe place to harden and dry.

**7** When the bracelet is completely dry, paint it silver. Cover the work surface if necessary. Leave the bracelet to dry again – then try it on!

# Art and Music

VIKING SINGING was, by all accounts, a drunken racket that was best avoided! However there must have been skilled Viking musicians, for writers mention fiddles, harps and horns. Musical instruments that have survived include simple flutes made of bone and panpipes made of wood.

In an age when few people could read or write, pictures were often used to tell stories. Pieces of tapestry survive from the Oseberg ship burial. They show a procession of horses and wagons. It is thought that they were woven by noble women. The tradition of making tapestries and embroideries to tell stories and events was continued by the Normans. The Bayeux tapestry was a typical sort of picture story. It celebrated the Norman conquest of England.

The Vikings rarely painted pictures. Art made by the Vikings was mostly carved on wooden panels or stones, or worked in metal. These often show bold, powerful figures, intricate patterns and graceful animals. They demonstrate the Viking artists' love of movement and line.

After the Viking Age, this distinctly Scandinavian style of art disappeared as Europeans brought different styles of art to the area.

**TWILIGHT OF THE GODS**
This stone carving from the Isle of Man shows the final battle of the gods. Odin, the father of the gods, is shown here armed with a spear and a raven on his shoulder. He is killed by Fenrir, the grey wolf.

**ART FROM URNES**
At Urnes, in Norway, there is a stave church that has old wood panels. They date from the final years of the Viking Age. This one shows a deer eating Yggdrasil, the tree that holds up the world. Urnes has given its name to the last and most graceful period of Viking art and design.

**MAKE A SCARY FACE**

*You will need: pencil, paper, scissors, self-drying clay, rolling pin, board, modelling tool, sandpaper, thick brush, acrylic paints, fine brush, water pot.*

**1** Draw a scary monster face on paper. Copy this one or one from a book, or make up your own. Make your drawing big and bold. Then cut it out.

**2** Roll out a large piece of modelling clay into a slab. Use a modelling tool to trim off the edges to look like the uneven shape of a rune stone.

**3** Lay your design on top of the clay slab. Use a modelling tool to go over the lines of your drawing, pushing through the paper into the clay.

## WOLF BITES GOD

This picture shows Tyr, god of the assemblies and law-makers. His hand is being bitten off by Fenrir, the grey wolf. Fenrir is straining against a magic chain forged by the dwarfs. The chain is made from all sorts of impossible things, such as fish's breath and a mountain's roots. Tyr's name survives in the English word 'Tuesday'.

## WHISTLE

This tiny whistle was made from a bird's leg bone. It may have been used to scare birds away from the crops.

## WALL HANGING

This boldly designed tapestry shows the gods Odin, Thor and Frey. It comes from a church in Sweden and dates from the 1100s, just after the Viking Age. It is probably similar to the wall hangings woven for royal halls in the earlier Viking times.

**4** Go over all the lines in the picture. Make sure the lines show up on the clay below. Remove the paper to see the monster's outline in clay.

**5** Leave the clay to dry, turning it over to make sure it is well aired. When it is hard, smooth it down with fine sandpaper, then brush with a paintbrush.

**6** Now paint the face as shown, using yellow ochre, black, red and blue. Let each colour dry completely before starting the next. Leave to dry.

*Here's a face to scare off evil spirits on a dark night! Faces like this, with interlacing beard and moustache, appeared on stone memorials in the Viking Age.*

# Ways of Writing

The Vikings developed their own ways of writing. Their alphabet was called the *futhark* after its seven opening letters. All runes (letters) are made up of straight lines and diagonals, because they were designed to be cut into wood, metal or stone. Most runes have survived on stone memorials, which are known as runestones. Historians believe that the Vikings thought the runes, or the runestones themselves, had their own magic. Some Vikings inlaid runes on their sword blades.

It takes a long time to carve runes, so they were only used for short messages. When Christianity came to the Viking lands, the monks needed to write out their holy scriptures. The text was too long to fit onto small bits of wood, so ink and paints were used on a vellum, or calfskin, surface. This was the method that other parts of Europe had been using for some time. There were only 16 runes, and so it had never been a very useful way to communicate. Eventually, the monks began to use the full Roman alphabet instead.

**TALES OF EIRIK**
The tales of Eirik the Red and his adventures were not written down or carved in runes, in his day. In about 1320 the stories, which had been passed down by word of mouth, were copied out in rather sooty ink on vellum which has darkened with age.

**RUNIC ALPHABET**
These are the 16 runes used by Danish Vikings. The Norwegian and Swedish version was slightly different.

## MAKE YOUR OWN RUNESTONE

*You will need: card, pencil, rolling pin, board, self-drying clay, modelling tool, PVA glue and brush, scissors, red acrylic paint, paintbrush, water pot, soft cloths.*

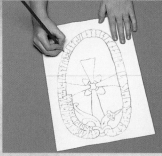

**1** Draw the outline of a runestone on card. Draw a line about 5cm in from the edge to make a border. Draw a cross in the middle as shown.

**2** Cut out the stone shape. Roll out the clay and lay the card runestone on it. Cut out a neat shape, as above, or leave as a natural-looking runestone, as in picture 5.

**3** Cut the border and the cross shape out of the card. Place the card border over the clay and draw round the inside edge of the border, as shown above.

## A VIKING HISTORY

Harald Finehair's Saga was copied out by hand in 1825, some 435 years after this ruler of Vestfold became the first king of all Norway. The text tells the story of the Viking kings. Although this new tradition of recording events on manuscript became popular, runes were used in Scandinavia well into the Middle Ages.

## THE NEW WRITING

As the Viking age drew to a close, skins of sheep, and of calves (vellum) began to be used for writing on. Words could be written down with a quill – the cut end of a feather – and ink. This was easier than carving runes into a stone.

*ink*

*vellum*

## RUNESTONE

Runestones have been found all over the Viking world. Years of rain and wind have worn them down. They have washed away the bright colours with which they were once painted. Even so, they tell us a great deal about the words and language that were used during the Viking Age.

## CELEBRATION

Vikings celebrated the glory of their dead relatives by raising memorial stones in public places. This runestone was put up by Varin for his son Vemod.

*Runestones often featured both pictures and writing.*

**4** Place the card cross shape on the clay. Draw round it with a modelling tool to make an indentation in the clay. Finally, cut runic letters into the clay border.

**5** Leave the clay to dry until it is completely hard and has gone pale. Then brush watered down PVA glue all over the slab, as shown above.

**6** Brush paint over the clay so that it sinks into the indents you have made with the modelling tool. The runes, the border and the cross should stand out.

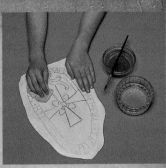

**7** Wipe the clay gently with a damp cloth, to remove all the paint, except in the indents. Leave to dry. Polish with a dry cloth.

# Stories and Riddles

A S THE VIKINGS sat around the fire, they told tales about feuds, battles, gods and the histories of their kings. These sagas, or stories, were passed down by word of mouth from one generation to the next. A typical adventure in one saga tells how Harald Hardradi fled from Constantinople. The Empress had ordered chains to be placed across the stretch of water where the ships were anchored. This was to stop the Vikings escaping. The Vikings rowed full tilt towards the chains. At the last moment some of the crew ran to the stern. This made the prow lift out of the water. The boat see-sawed over the chains and sailed away!

Poets called *skålds* travelled from hall to hall. They were expected to sing the praises of their host. If the king or jarl liked the verses, the poet was well rewarded. If he did not like them, the poet's life could be at risk. Poets loved to include riddles in their verses. For example, 'a marvel with eight feet, four eyes and knees higher than its body' was a spider. The audience had to guess what it was.

**THE FINAL BATTLE**
This wooden panel tells the story of the last great battle between the gods and the giants. Odin leads the charge against the wolf Fenrir, but is gulped down in the beast's huge jaws.

**WRITING IT ALL DOWN**
This capital letter has been beautifully decorated. It shows the real life King Harald Finehair cutting the chains of a mythical giant called Dofri. It comes from a book that was made after the Viking Age. Stories that had been told by word of mouth during the Viking years were at last written down as sagas.

**THE STORY OF SIGURD**
Many magical stories were told about an ancient hero named Sigurd. This fine wood carving from the 1100s shows Sigurd slaying a dragon with his great sword. In his other hand he carries a Norman shield.

## TOMBSTONE TALES

Ancient Scandinavian myths and legends remained popular well into the Christian period. This is a reconstruction of a tombstone dating from about 1030. Historians believe that it may show a lion in a battle with a serpent. The stone was found in the churchyard of St Paul's Cathedral in England. Archaeologists can imagine how the original tombstone may have looked by the traces of paint left on it. It is thought that the colours on this reconstruction are not very accurate.

## THE POET'S REWARD

This massive silver bracelet comes from Falster in Denmark. A skåld might well have received a bracelet like this, or a ring, if the jarl enjoyed the tales that he told in the chieftain's hall.

## THE SERPENT OF MIDGARD

In this picture a gigantic monster called the serpent of Midgard thrashes the sea. It is in battle with the hammer-bearing god Thor. The old stories of the Vikings describe the doom of the gods and the destruction of the world. Only when the world is destroyed can a new world be born.

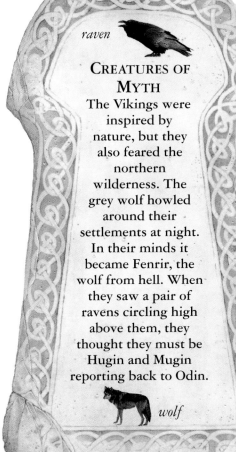

raven

## CREATURES OF MYTH

The Vikings were inspired by nature, but they also feared the northern wilderness. The grey wolf howled around their settlements at night. In their minds it became Fenrir, the wolf from hell. When they saw a pair of ravens circling high above them, they thought they must be Hugin and Mugin reporting back to Odin.

wolf

# Leisure Pursuits

T HE VIKINGS LOVED life. They raced their ships and even tried to run along the oars while the boat was being rowed. Children and adults enjoyed swimming and wrestling, as well as archery, swordplay and weightlifting. Skating and skiing were pastimes as well as means of transport.

Icelanders met up at horse fairs and enjoyed betting on fights between wild ponies. They hunted for pleasure as well as to bring home food. Like their Arab trading partners, the Vikings loved falconry. Wild falcons became a valuable export from the settlements in Greenland. The Vikings used birds of prey to hunt hares and other small animals and birds. Hunting dogs were used as retrievers to collect prey caught by a falcon or hawk.

Festivals were a chance to feast and to forget the northern cold and darkness. The Vikings celebrated midwinter, the coming of summer and the harvest. Evenings by the fire could be taken up with playing dice, or with a board game called *hnefatafl*. In this game, one player had to protect the king from the pieces of the other player. Some boards were beautifully made, while others were very simple. The Vikings also learned how to play the game of chess when they traded in the cities of the Middle East.

### GET YOUR SKATES ON

These Viking skates are made of soft leather and were found by archaeologists in York. They have a smooth blade made from an animal bone. Sweden has thousands of lakes that freeze over in winter, and the Vikings were very good skaters. They sometimes used poles to push themselves along.

### CHECKMATE!

The pieces in this Viking chess set are made of walrus ivory. They date from the 1100s. The complete chess set was found on the Isle of Lewis, off the west coast of Scotland.

### MAKE A HNEFATAFL BOARD

*You will need: self-drying clay, rolling pin, board, modelling tool, ruler, sandpaper, water pot, PVA glue and brush, acrylic paints, paintbrush.*

1 Take a large block of red modelling clay. Roll it out flat to cover as large an area as possible without rolling it too thin. Be sure to roll the clay evenly.

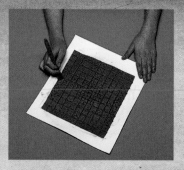

2 Trim the clay to a square, as shown. Score lines on the board, to make 11 x 11 squares. Use your modelling tool to make crosses on the outside and central squares.

3 Sand the board. Give it a coat of watered down glue and leave to dry. Paint the central squares with yellow ochre and the outer squares red. Leave to dry.

## DICE

One of these dice is made from bone, the other from walrus ivory. Holes have been drilled to mark the spots on the dice. The Vikings loved board games. Long ago, these dice would have been rattling on a bench or table in the chieftain's hall.

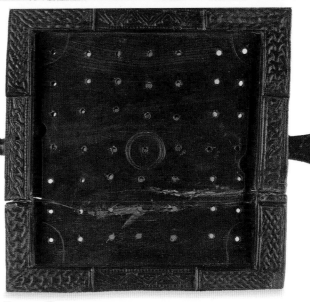

## IRISH GAMES

This games board comes from Ballinderry in Ireland. It may have been used for playing hnefatafl. The Vikings loved gambling and all kinds of games.

## PRIZED FALCONS

The Bayeux tapestry shows a falconer wading on board King Harold's ship. Falconry was one of the most popular forms of hunting in Europe and would have been very familiar to Vikings and Normans.

*Hnefatafl was the Vikings' favourite board game for winter evenings. The pieces would have been made of chalk and amber.*

**4** Make nine clay playing pieces, of which one 'king' is bigger. When dry, paint the king and three other pieces black and paint five pieces white.

**5** Place the black king in the centre, surrounded by the other black pieces. Place the white pieces on the red patterned squares at the edges.

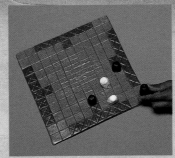

**6** Players take turns to move the pieces across the board. Hnefatafl is played rather like a game of chess or draughts. The aim is to take the king.

**7** Make up some rules for the game. Decide which way the pieces can move and by how many squares. Do not forget to decide how the game is won!

# Viking Burials

THE END of a Viking's life was marked with a funeral. Kings, queens and other rich Vikings were often buried with treasures to use in the next world. Sometimes slaves were killed and buried with them. Less wealthy Vikings might travel to the next world with their sword or the tools of their trade. The kings and queens of Denmark were buried in stone chambers inside great mounds at Jelling. Large runestones were raised as memorials to the dead. Relatives carved inscriptions on these stones, telling of the loved ones they had lost. In parts of the British Isles, Viking settlers took on the local custom of carving gravestones.

Seafaring was very important to the Viking way of life. As a result, the custom grew up of burying important people in splendid ships. People believed that the dead would use these ships to sail to the next world. Burial ships were usually buried under mounds, or sometimes they were set on fire at sea in a great, final blaze.

### FROM THE GRAVE
This fine bucket was found in a woman's grave at Birka, in Sweden. It is made of wood covered with bronze. It was probably made in the British Isles about 1,100 years ago.

### SHIP SHAPES
These stones were erected in the shape of a longship. They mark a Viking grave in Gotland, Sweden. Burial stones such as these are common throughout Scandinavia. These ship burial sites symbolize the idea of death as a voyage into the unknown.

## UP-HELLY-AA

At the end of January a festival is held in the Shetland Isles. A model Viking ship is set ablaze with flaming torches. It marks the end of the midwinter festival, Up-Helly-Aa. No one really knows the origin of this festival but one story by an Arab chronicler talks of a similar event, the burning of a Viking burial boat on the river Volga.

## THE GOKSTAD SHIP

This royal ship was excavated from a burial mound at Gokstad in 1880. It was rebuilt and can be seen today in the Viking Ship Museum at Bygdøy, Norway.

## GOODS
## FROM GRAVES

This beautiful silver cup was found in a royal burial mound at Jelling, in Denmark. It was probably buried with King Gorm, father of Harald Bluetooth, sometime around the year AD958. Although it is likely that King Gorm's body was buried with many other items, few remained when the tomb was excavated. It is likely that the chamber was entered hundreds of years ago and the goods mysteriously removed in an orderly fashion.

# GLOSSARY

## A

**aerial** From the air.

**alloy** A mixture of metals melted together to create a new substance.

**amber** The fossilized resin from pine trees. Amber was very highly prized by the Celts.

**amphora** A tall pottery jar used to store wine. Its plural is 'amphorae'.

**anvil** An iron block used for shaping metal.

**archaeologist** Someone who makes a scientific study of ancient remains and ruins.

## B

**barbarians** Wild, rough and uncivilized people. The word was invented by the ancient Greeks to describe people who did not speak their language or follow their lifestyle. The Greeks thought that the spoken languages of these people sounded like 'bar, bar'.

**bards** In Celtic times, bards were well-educated poets. Becoming a bard was the first stage in the long training to be a druid.

**berserkir** Viking warriors who worked themselves up into a frenzy of rage before battle. They were named after their bearskin cloaks or shirts.

**boar** A wild pig.

**brazier** A metal stand for holding burning coals.

**broch** A tall, round stone tower built by the Celts in Scotland. Brochs were probably originally built as safe places for people to shelter in wartime.

**bronze** A metal alloy, made from a mixture of copper and tin.

**brynja** A warrior's tunic made of iron rings, or mail.

**burial ship** Vikings were sometimes buried or cremated in finely decorated wooden ships.

**byre** A cowshed.

## C

**carnyx** A Celtic war trumpet.

**cauldron** A huge cooking pot.

**caulk** To seal the planks of a ship with tar or other material, so that it stays watertight.

**causeway** A raised walkway.

**chainmail** Small rings of metal, linked together to form a fine mesh, used to protect the body in battle.

**chalice** The ceremonial cup, often of silver or gold, used by Christian priests to hold wine.

**citadel** A stronghold.

**clans** Families who trace their descent from a single ancestor, and who share ties of loyalty and a family name.

## cliff castle
A Celtic fort and lookout post built on top of a cliff.

**colonize** To settle in a foreign land or colony.

**coracle** A small boat made of leather stretched across a wooden frame.

**crannog** Small, artificial islands that the Celts built in lakes.

**cremation** The process of burning dead bodies.

## D

**Danegeld** Money paid to Vikings by English or French rulers to prevent their being attacked.

**dictator** A ruler with unrestricted power.

**die** A tool for punching a design into metal.

**dismantled** Taken to pieces.

**distaff** A long stick used to hold wool while it is being spun.

**dowry** Money that is given to a newly-married couple, usually by the bride's father.

**drinking horn** The hollow horn of a cow, often decorated with silver and used as a drinking cup.

**druids** Celtic priests. According to Roman writers, there were three different grades of druid. Some studied the natural world and claimed to foretell the future. Some were bards who knew about history. Some led Celtic worship, made sacrifices to the gods, and administered holy laws.

## F

**faering** A small rowing boat used for fishing or coastal journeys.

**falconry** Using birds of prey to hunt other birds or animals.

**feud** A long-standing quarrel, especially between two families.

**firedogs** Ornamental metal props used to hold logs in place on an open fire.

**fjord** A deep sea inlet formed long ago by the action of ice. The Norwegian coast has many fjords.

**fort** A fortified military position. Viking forts had a strict geometrical layout. Each one lay within a high circular rampart of earth and turf.

## G

**graffiti** Words or pictures that have been scratched or written on to a wall, statue or other object.

**grid** A rectangular pattern made by straight lines crossing each other at right angles.

**gripping beast** A design used by Viking craft workers, in which animals or monsters are shown locked in combat.

## H

**Hallstatt era** The early part of the Celtic period, dated from around 750 to 450BC. It is named after a place in Austria.

**harness** The leather straps that are used to attach horses to chariots or other vehicles.

**Hedeby** An important Danish Viking town (now in Germany).

**hilt** The handle of a sword.

**hnefatafl** A popular boardgame played in Viking times.

**hoe** A sharp blade fitted to a long pole. It is used to kill weeds that are growing amongst crop plants.

## I

**imported** Brought from abroad.

**induce** To bring something about.

**iron ore** The rock that contains iron in a raw, natural form. Before the iron can be used, the ore has to be crushed and then heated to release the metal.

**iron-shod** Something that is bound with iron.

## J

**jarl** A Viking chieftain. The word is linked to the English 'earl'.

## K

**karl** A free-born Viking man, able to own land, trade and fight.

**keel** The long beam that supports the frame of a wooden ship, running along the base of the hull.

**knarr** A sturdy trading ship, designed to carry cargo.

**krater** A large ancient Greek bowl used for mixing wine and water together.

## L

**La Tène era** The late part of the Celtic period, dated from around 450 to 50BC.

**latticed** In a criss-cross pattern.

**Law Speaker** The person who read out the laws passed by the assembly of free Vikings.

**longhouse** The chief building of a Viking farmstead, including a great hall.

**longship** A long, seagoing vessel used by the Vikings for warfare or exploration.

**loom** A wooden frame used for weaving cloth.

**lyre** An ancient musical instrument that is played by plucking its strings.

## M

**marl** Natural lime, dug from under the ground.

**mead** An alcoholic drink made from honey.

**mercenary** A soldier who hires out his services to an army for money.

**midden** A rubbish tip or dunghill.

**Midgard** Vikings believed that Midgard was the human world.

**missionary** Someone who tries to convert others to their own religious beliefs.

**molten** Something that is melted.

**myth** Any ancient story about gods, magic and imaginary places.

## N

**nasal** A metal bar fitted to a helmet to protect the nose.

**Norman** A descendant of the Vikings who settled in northern France.

## O

**Odin** The most powerful and mysterious god. He was the god of war, magic and poetry.

**Ogham** The Celtic writing system, based on the Latin alphabet.

**oppida** The Roman name for Celtic towns.

## P

**pagan** Pre-Christian, worshipping the old gods of nature and the countryside.

**parasite** In Celtic times, the low-ranking follower of a chieftain. His duty was to praise the chieftain, especially before a battle.

**pedestal** A stand that supports an object.

**pewter** An alloy, or mixture of metals, made from tin and lead.

**Picts** A mysterious people who lived in Scotland from about AD300 to AD900. They were descended from earlier Celts.

**picture stone** A memorial stone carved with pictures.

**plunder** Stolen goods.

**prow** The front end of a ship. Longship prows were often carved with dragon heads.

## Q

**quern** A simple machine, made from two stones, that is used to grind corn for flour.

## R

**ramparts** Steep earth banks.

**relics** Items associated with famous or holy people.

**reliquary** A container for holy objects such as relics.

**repoussé** A metalworking technique that is used to create decorative raised patterns on a metal object.

**republic** A land that is not ruled by a king, queen or emperor.

**reputedly** According to legend or unconfirmed reports.

**rigging** The ropes used to support a ship's mast and sails.

**rune** One of the symbols made up of lines, used as letters of the alphabet by the peoples of ancient Germany and Scandinavia.

**runestone** A memorial stone carved with runes.

**Rus** The name given to Swedish traders who settled in eastern Europe.

## S

**saga** A family history or heroic tale told by storytellers in old Scandinavia or Iceland.

**scabbard** The container for a sword-blade. It is usually fixed to a belt.

**severed** Cut off.

**shield boss** The metal plate that is fixed to the centre of a shield in order to protect the hand of the person holding the shield.

**shift** A plain, straight and very simple dress.

**shrine** A holy place where gods are worshipped.

**sickle** A large, sharp curved knife.

**skáld** A Viking poet, storyteller and inventor of riddles.

**spindle** A whirling tool used to make fibre, such as wool, into yarn for weaving.

**slats** Strips of wood.

**soldered** Something that is joined together with small pieces of melted metal.

**spatula** A blunt knife used for scooping and spreading.

**standard-bearer** A soldier who carries an army's flag or emblem (special badge) into battle.

**status symbols** Signs of wealth and power.

**stave** A plank made from splitting a tree trunk.

**stern** The rear end of a ship.

**strake** One of the long, overlapping planks running along the side of a longship.

**sumptuous** Rich and splendid.

## T

**talisman** A lucky charm.

**tapestry** A cloth with a picture or design woven by hand on its threads.

**terret ring** A ring that is fixed to a chariot, through which reins pass.

**Thing** An assembly of free men, which passed laws in Viking lands. The Icelandic assembly was called the Althing.

**Thor** The fierce, red-bearded god of thunder.

**thrall** A slave.

**torc** A heavy necklace. The Celts believed that torcs had magic, protective powers.

**trance** The state of being asleep yet conscious.

**treasure hoard** A stash of treasure buried for safe-keeping.

**tribe** A group of families who owe loyalty to a chief.

**triumphal arch** A large archway, built to honour a conquering army and its commander on their return from war.

## V

**Valholl** or **Valhalla** The great hall of the gods, where brave Viking warriors were welcomed after death.

**valkyrie** In Viking myths, the valkyrie was one of Odin's female attendants, who welcomed heroes to Valholl. She was sometimes shown as an old hag who hovered over battlefields like a vulture.

**vallus** The Roman name for a Celtic farm machine, used for reaping (cutting) grain crops.

**vane** A light metal plate used to show the direction of the wind.

**Viking** One of the Scandinavian peoples who lived by sea-raiding in the early Middle Ages.

**Vinland** The name given by the Vikings to part of the North American coast (Newfoundland).

## W

**wagons** Carved wooden carts, sometimes used in burials as coffins.

**wattle and daub** A building material made from woven twigs and branches covered with a paste made of clay, mud and sometimes animal dung.

**woad** A blue dye, made from plants, used by the Celts to paint or tattoo their skin.

# INDEX